ENCOURAGE

Roger Gulick

Edited by Paul R. Keating

**A Daily Devotional
to encourage and challenge**

Dedication

This book is dedicated with admiration and affection to the outstanding staff of Entrust, the mission my wife and I have worked with throughout the world these last sixteen years.

It is also dedicated to my wife, Joy, who has been my perfect partner in ministry for over half a century.

CONTENTS

You Got an "A"	1
Accessing God's Power and Wisdom	3
We Are Citizen of Another World	6
Count Your Many Blessings	9
Don't Worry About Anything	11
A Prayer for All Christians	13
For This I Need Jesus	16
Grow Where You Are Planted	18
How to Keep Close to the Lord	20
Hungering and Thirsting	23
Is It All Up to You?	26
Keep Plugged In	28
My Joy Isn't to Produce	31
Our Eternal Tender	34
Plus Ultra	36
Take Time to Smell the Roses	38
The Duck Tape Wallet	40
The Power of Poetry	43
Who Are You?	45
Your Ministry May Produce Giants of Faith	49
Worrying Without Ceasing Versus Praying Without Ceasing	53
God Was Here	55
Speaking as a Resident Alien	57
The Balanced Christian Life	59
The Lord Gives Strength to His People	61
When Troubles Hit	65
A Blessing of Salvation: Hope	68
All Your Earthly Possessions in a Nine Year Old Ford	71
Are You Excited About Heaven?	73
Christian Hope Is Not Just Hoping	76
Contentment…or Not	79

ENCOURAGE

Count Your Many Blessings	81
Courtesy to a Grumpy Salesclerk	83
Diamonds in the Rough	85
Encouragement in the Midst of Financial Troubles	87
Glorifying God when the Storms Hit	89
God's Surprising Sovereignty	91
God's Will and Opposition	93
His Eye Is on the Sparrow	95
How Could I Do Such a Thing?	97
How Not to Grow Weary in Well Doing	99
I Just Choose to Be Happy	101
Why Did You Doubt?	104
Especially Need Encouragement?	106
What Life Are You Waiting For?	118
Living the Hidden Life	110
Looking Not Just to Our Own Interests	112
On Breaking Bruised Reeds	114
I'm Working Hard. Why Don't Things Work Out?	116
Protecting Our Children from God	119
The Church of Jesus Christ is on the Move	122
The Kingdom of God and Hardships	125
Trusting that God Is Good	127
Ugly Brown Stains	129
When Troubles Come	131
Biblical Virtues	133
God's Unscheduled Opportunities	137
Attitude	139
A Leader's Prayer	141
Walking on Water	143
Abide with Me	145
Plenteous Redemption	147

ENCOURAGE

You Got an "A"

It is amazing how protective most parents are with their children.

Once I saw a fifth grade boy throw a stone at my third grade daughter. I chased him two blocks and caught him. Happily, the kid mistakenly thought I, a thirty-something old man, could never catch him. But that was my daughter!

Steve Brown, homiletics professor at Reformed Seminary, tells how he once sought to protect his daughter when she was a high school senior. She had signed up for several advanced and difficult courses. After classes began however, she realized that taking all those courses was going to be too much for her. She decided to drop one tough course. The teacher of that class had a reputation of being tough in every way. Steve's daughter was terrified just to ask permission to drop the class. So she asked her father to go with her. Steve, being a loving and protective dad, of course, agreed.

The next morning the two of them had an appointment with "Mrs. Toughguy." Being the protective father, Steve explained to the teacher that his daughter thought it would be best if she dropped the class. The teacher did not answer Steve, but turned to the daughter and kindly asked her why she thought she should drop the class. Steve's daughter responded that though she would like to continue with the class, she thought it would be too difficult to get the grade she needed to keep up her grade point average.

The teacher opened her grade book to Steve's daughter's name and wrote in a final grade: "A".

She said softly, "Young lady, that is your final grade. It's in ink and will not be changed. Do you still want to leave my class?"

Of course, she stayed. And Steve learned a great lesson about grace from that wise teacher.

A friend once commented to me that for most of his life he has thought of being justified by God's grace and keeping that justification and keeping God pleased with him by his own works. I too have discovered that kind of thinking as I have sought to live out my Christian life. Have I done enough for God? Is he displeased with me? Does He look down on me like a disapproving father and shake his head and frown?

I need to remember, not just in my head, but at the center of my being that, because of what Jesus did on the cross, I have an "A" in God's grade book. My goal in life is not to win God's favor by working hard. I already have an "A". He won't love me more and give me a better grade if I am really successful. I already have an "A". He won't love me less and lower my grade if I sometimes trip and fall. I already have an "A" written in Jesus' blood in the Book of Life.

So…how do you think Steve's daughter did in that course? Do you think she goofed off and didn't do the homework because she already had a 100? I really don't know. Steve didn't speak of that, but I think I know what happened. I think I know, because I know what happens to me when I understand and incorporate into my life the reality of God's grace and the 100 he has provided for me. That knowing frees me from the burden and pressure of performing to keep God happy. Nor does God's grace motivate me to goof off or be casual about living a Christ-like life. Rather, it motivates me to do my best out of love and gratitude. How freeing that is; how encouraging, for you too.

A question to think about before you close this book today:

What do I believe God thinks about me? How does that impact the way I live?

ENCOURAGE

Accessing God's Power and Wisdom

Every time a new year begins I get excited about what God has ahead for me. But I know living for Christ in today's world will not be easy. I am going to need help from someone stronger and wiser than I am. God fits that requirement. He is all powerful and all wise. Now my problem is: How do I tie in with his power and wisdom? By experience I know it is not automatic that every believer gets God's peace when they're panicking and finds endurance when they're empty and finds courage when they're cowardly, God certainly can help us with the will power to avoid doing things we shouldn't do and do the things we know we should do. But the big question is: How do we access his power when tragedy strikes, when we're lured by temptation, or when we want to grow in Christ-likeness? I want to mention several things that help me. You probably already know all this, but I have discovered that it is good to be reminded of things we know but don't always remember to put into practice.

I Chronicles 16:11-12 says, *"Look to the Lord and his strength; seek his face always. Remember the wonders he has done, his miracles."* I have found it helpful to take time to think back and **remember situations when God has come through in wonderful ways.** For the last few years Joy has been writing down stories she remembers of God's working in our lives. We have found that just remembering those things has been very encouraging and strengthening.

Reading Christian biographies has also helped me think about the wonders God has done. Through their stories I am reminded that God is not some distant, detached and disinterested deity. He was a very powerful and real presence in those people's lives and he can be that in mine and in yours. Get a good Christian biography and start reading.

Second we need to admit our own weakness. So often when a difficulty or a temptation comes, our reaction is to try to get through it on our own. The reality is that we cannot be filled with the power of God until we first empty ourselves of the pretense that we can make it through on our own. God can only fill empty vessels. When we admit our helplessness and weakness, we open ourselves for God power to fill us.

Thirdly, we need align ourselves with God's will. Some people think God's power is like an electrical outlet that we plug into when we feel we are a bit over our heads and need God's help. But God's power doesn't work that way. Jesus said in John 15:5, *"I'm the vine, you are the branches. Whoever remains in me and I in him will bear much fruit."* There is a big difference between an electric cord plugged into a wall outlet and a branch connected to a vine. Moment by moment we need to be connected with God as a branch is to the vine. Align yourself with God's will and walk down the road God wants you to walk on. Then as you keep putting one foot in front of the other, God will give you strength to take the next step.

Fourthly, ask God for the power we need. The Bible tells us, *"You have not because you ask not."* We cannot move through life just assuming God is going to take care of us and give us the strength we need to face whatever comes. Stay in close touch with God. If you humbly ask for help and guidance in a situation, He will give it.

The fifth step may be the most important: **act right now in obedience to God.** There's a pattern in scripture that even if we don't feel empowered, we're still to take action by obediently proceeding on the road God wants us to walk. As we do he promises to give us strength as strength is needed. When we do that, we are demonstrating faith. Faith is not just believing some facts. Faith is belief plus behavior, belief plus actions. Faith is almost always a verb in the Bible, not a noun. Someone said that if you were taking a picture of faith it would come out blurred because it would be moving as you took the picture.

Some of you have read the book God's Smuggler, by Brother Andrew. During the Cold War days, he believed God had called him to get Bibles to people behind the Iron Curtain who desperately wanted them but could not get them. He said, "Here's how it happened. I would pray and would sense God leading me to a particular country, a closed society. My advisors would pray too and we would come to an agreement, 'Yes, this is the country God wants us to bring Bibles into.' When we came to that realization, I often didn't feel great boldness, or tremendous courage, I was scared stiff. I didn't feel like God had suddenly infused me with a great ability or great power or courage. What I would do is walk in obedience down the road toward the border of that country with the Bibles. Time after time in the most amazing way the door to that country would swing open and God would find a way for me to get those Bibles into that country. God gave the strength to do it, the power to do it, the ability to do it as I needed it along the way of obedience."

He continued "It's sort of like a supermarket door. If you're sitting in the parking lot at a supermarket and look at the door, you could sit there all day and wish and hope but the door is not going to open as a result of you mentally trying to make it open. But if you begin to walk toward that door in faith, you know you're not going to bump into that door because as you approach the door there's a sensor that will know you're approaching and the door is going to open. It opens because you're walking in faith toward the door. That's basically the principle I've lived by all these years. God is waiting for us to walk forward in obedience so he can open the door for us to serve him."

Is there an area in your life where you've gone through the first four steps of how to receive God's power, but you're still afraid? I would say, take action. When we demonstrate faith by taking specific steps of obedience, even when we don't feel empowered by God, he will give us what we need.

Be encouraged. Remember, that all powerful God is your Father.

A question to think about before you close this book today:

When was the last time I stepped out over my head and did something where I knew I would fall flat on my face unless God came through?

We Are Citizens of Another World

I remember when Ronald Reagan defeated Jimmy Carter in 1980. Both were Christian men, though Carter was much more outspoken and even taught a weekly Sunday School class. Carter had been a success in everything he had done but told Philip Yancey that when he lost the election he returned to Plaines, Georgia, a broken man, scorned even by fellow Democrats. Have you ever felt broken? His family business, held in a blind trust during his term, had accumulated a million-dollar debt. Ever been in debt?

He slowly began to rebuild. He wrote a book that helped pay off debts, He started a center in Atlanta to foster programs he believed in. His long emphasis on human rights opened up opportunities to monitor elections all over the world. His support of Habitat for Humanity helped the new ministry to grow. His foundation targeted some major diseases that plague poor nations and now both guinea worm and river blindness have nearly been eliminated.

He still teaches Sunday School in the little church he attends. Every other month he takes his turn in mowing the church lawn and Rosalynn cleans the bathrooms. Yancey wrote "He keeps cranking out books, hammering nails for Habitat, judging elections. Rosalynn champions the causes of childhood immunization and treatment for mental illness. Together, they seem like the ideal small-town citizens, if you forget for a moment that they used to entertain kings and queens and slept next to a briefcase with nuclear codes that could destroy the planet."

Carter's reputation came back. In 2002 he received possibly the most prestigious honor on earth, the Nobel Peace Prize. He is far from perfect but is probably one of the most admired ex-presidents. Other presidents have gone on to major on golf or their celebrity status. The Carters have given themselves to service of others. They have lived in the "real" world, but have kept their eyes on the REAL world.

It reminds me of Jesus' words, "For whoever wants to save his life will lose it, but whoever loses his life for me and for the gospel will save it." My friends, we are called to live life in two worlds, the physical and the spiritual. This physical world is always with us and "we absorb its surrounding culture by osmosis." It says youth, beauty, wealth, popularity, and success are what counts. But Jesus came to earth, in part, to show us how to look at life from a different perspective. Paul wrote, "Set your minds on things above, not on earthly things" (Col.3:2) and "regard no one from a worldly point of view" (2 Cor. 5:16).

Christ followers need to learn to look at the world upside down. Probable some of you have chosen a vocation that doesn't pay as much as you could get with one that might cause you to compromise some of your values. Many of you have chosen to live a more moderate lifestyle so you could give more to build the kingdom of God. You might be tempted at times to look at people living in larger houses with high paying jobs and envy them. But we don't just live in this world. We are citizens of another world.

Frederick Buechner wrote, "*If the world is sane, then Jesus is mad as a hatter and the Last Supper is the Mad Tea Party. The world says, Mind your own business and Jesus says: There is no such thing as your own business. The world says, Follow the wisest course and be a success and Jesus says, Follow me and be crucified. The world says, Drive carefully – the life you save may be your own – and Jesus says, Whoever would save his life will lose it, and whoever loses his life for my sake will find it.*

"*The world says, Law and order, and Jesus says, Love. The world says, Get, and Jesus says, Give. In terms of the world's sanity, Jesus is as crazy as a coot, and anybody who thinks he can follow him without being a little crazy too is laboring less under the cross than under a delusion.* "We are fools for Christ's sake." Paul says, faith says, the foolishness of God is *wiser than the wisdom of men, the lunacy of Jesus is saner that the grim sanity of the world."*

My dear crazy friends, enjoy your craziness. The world really doesn't have a clue. What it values and prizes in reality are nothing, just vanity of vanities.

Be encouraged.

A question to think about before you close this book today:

The world says, "Get," and Jesus says, "Give." What do you have to give?

Count Your Many Blessings

In reading one of Max Lucado's books I found a story that encouraged and challenged me.

A short term missionary worked for a while in a leper colony. On his final day there, he was leading worship. He asked if anyone had a favorite song. He noticed a woman in the congregation, a leper, who had the most disfigured face he'd ever seen. She had no ears and no nose; her lips were gone. Slowly she raised a fingerless hand and asked, "Can we sing, 'Count Your Many Blessings'?"

Are we ready to do that today? Are you ready to sing "Count Your Many Blessings"? Actually all of us have many more blessings than that leper. We could and should sing that song every day.

Psalm 23 reminds us: THE LORD IS MY SHEPHERD; I SHALL NOT WANT. That is absolutely true. We have a good shepherd who will meet all our needs. No matter what we are experiencing today, along with that leper we can sing "Count Your Many Blessings." If we get down at times, it is not that we need a change in our circumstances so our attitude is better. If we think like that, we are in the prison of want. We have forgotten that all we need we have in our Shepherd.

What is the one thing separating us from joy? How would you fill in this blank: I will be happy when...? When I am healed? When I am thinner? When I have another child? When my children leave home? When I have more money? When our staff is perfect?

Now, with that answer firmly in mind, answer this. If your ship never comes in, if your dream never comes true, if the situation never changes, could you be happy? If you, if we, cannot be, then we are sleeping in the cold cell of discontent. We are in the prison of want. We need to remember all that we have in our Shepherd.

We have a loving God who hears us, the power of love behind us, the Holy Spirit within us, and all of heaven ahead of us. If we have the Good Shepherd, we have grace for every sin, direction for every turn, a candle for every corner, and an anchor for every storm. We have everything we need.

And who can take it from us? Can cancer infect our salvation? Can financial crises impoverish our prayers? A hurricane might take our earthly house, but it won't touch our heavenly home. Isn't that great!

Let's get out our hymnbooks and sing "Count Your Many *Blessings*".

A question to do before you close this book today:

Fill in the blank: I will be happy when:

Don't Worry About Anything?

I was in a discussion group the other day that was considering Matthew 6:25.

"Therefore I tell you, do not worry about your life, what you will eat or drink or about your body, what you will wear."

Someone pointed out that Philippians 4:6 uses the same Greek word for *worry* but translates it there as anxious: *"Do not be anxious about anything...."* Then a businessman who had gone through some difficult times asked, "How can an intelligent person not ever worry. Life is full of hard times: illnesses, children not following the Lord, accidents, divorce, bankruptcy, Christian friends letting us down, business partners cheating us, and a lot more." He's right, so why does Jesus tell us not to worry and Paul tell us not to be anxious *about anything*? Did Jesus and Paul not live in the same world as we do?

I would guess that some of you have faced, or are facing difficult situations that my friend never even thought about. Now, did Jesus and Paul really mean what they said: *Don't worry about anything*? Nothing seems more natural in this world than to be anxious, to be burdened, to worry.

But Jesus then told us why we need not worry, *"...do not worry about what you will eat or drink...or about what you will wear... Is not life more important than food, and the body more important than clothes?"* What's he saying there? If we think about it a bit, we will realize that it is a profound and powerful argument. Our life that we are worrying about, how did we get it? This body with its aches and pains that we are anxious about, where did it come from? We are alive right now because God wills it and decides it. And our body also is a gift from God. The argument that Jesus used is that if God has given us the gift of life, do you think He will not see to it that our life is sustained? Since God has given us our body, we can be quite certain that he will provide the means by which we can be clothed? It is an argument from the greater to the lesser. He did the greater thing, giving us life, will he not to the smaller thing, sustain it?

ENCOURAGE

A few verses later in our text Jesus calls those who worry, *those of little faith.* By this he means we fail to think as we should. We fail to realize that God is the giver of our life and our body and there is a plan for every life in the mind of God. We can be certain that God has a plan and a purpose for our lives and it will be carried out. So we need never be anxious when bad things happen or when we think they might happen. God is sovereign. There are no accidents in a Christian's life.

This truth is what kept the great heroes of the faith going (Hebrews 11). They might not have understood what was going on, but they had confidence that God knew, and that "He who brought them into being and had a purpose for them, would not leave nor forsake them. He would surely sustain and lead them all the journey through, until their purpose in this world had been completed, and…then He would receive them into his presence." Martyn Lloyd-Jones The Sermon on the Mount, pg. 386.

Also worrying or being anxious is not the same as being concerned about something. Paul was concerned that the young churches in Galatia not *"turn to another gospel."* Jesus was not happy about going to the cross. In the Garden he said to his friends, *"My soul is overwhelmed with sorrow to the point of death."* Paul could have had a much easier life had he just stopped preaching the gospel. "If I keep this up, I very well might be stoned, ship wrecked, beaten with rods, in danger from bandits, go without sleep, know hunger and thirst and end up in prison." But apparently neither Jesus' sorrow nor Paul's concern about the young churches nor his awareness of coming hard times were what the Bible means by worry or anxiety. The faith that kept them going and keeps us going is our confidence that God knows what he is doing and has a purpose in it all.

I trust this thought encourages you. Otherwise you might be like a friend of mine who said, "I think this situation is too big for God. I'll start worrying and that will take care of it."

A question to think about before you close this book today: What is causing me to worry/be anxious right now? What can/should I do about it?

A Prayer for All Christians

The first Global Day of Prayer was in the spring of 2005. It was estimated that over 200 million followers of Christ from over 150 countries participated. Since then this has been an annual event. Below is the prayer that everyone used on that first Global Day of Prayer. Take some time and pray through this prayer and rejoice that millions of people believe this way and that they are your brothers and sisters in Christ. That is something to be encouraged about.

Almighty God, Father, Son and Holy Spirit, as a united worldwide Body of believers, we are gathered today to honor and glorify Your Name. We bow before Your throne of grace and acknowledge that You are the Creator of heaven and earth. You existed through all eternity and in you all things hold together. There is no one like You, holy and righteous in all Your ways. We submit to Your authority and sovereignty as the King of the universe and pray with one voice to enthrone You in our hearts and to honor You before the world.

Lord God, You alone are worthy of our praise and adoration. We worship You.

Our Father in heaven, thank You for loving the world so greatly that You gave Your only Son, Jesus Christ, to die on the cross for our sins, so that we could be reconciled to You. Thank You for giving us the right to call You Father, because of our faith in Jesus Christ as our Savior. Nothing, not even principalities and powers, is able to separate us from your love, which you demonstrated in your Son, Jesus Christ.

Thank you, Father, for adopting us into Your family. We now cry, Abba Father.

Lord Jesus Christ, You alone are worthy to open the scrolls of history for You were slain and have redeemed us to the Father by Your blood. Thank You for interceding for us as our High Priest. As we stand before You from many tribes and nations, we confess that You are Head of the Church and Lord of every created thing in heaven and on earth. Come and

ENCOURAGE

draw followers to serve you from every tribe and language. May these become Your inheritance in every nation of this world. Let Your Kingdom be established in every nation of this world so that governments will rule with righteousness and justice. May Your gospel be made known to every person on earth. May Your blessing bring transformation amidst every people on earth. And may Your glory cover the earth as the waters cover the seas.

Lord Jesus Christ, we confess that You are our Savior.

Father of mercy and grace, we acknowledge that we have sinned and that our world is gripped by the power of sin. Our hearts are grieved by the injustice and hatred, the bloodshed, violence, anger, resentment, racism, oppression, greed and selfishness. We weep because of the loss of innocent lives in war and terrorism, abortion and senseless murders. Our hearts are broken by every rejection of Christ as Lord and Savior. We come before Your throne of grace and ask for mercy and help.

God of mercy, please pour out Your grace and forgive us for our sins.

Spirit of the living God, we confess that we can do nothing apart from You. Living God, on this Pentecost, pour out Your Spirit on all flesh. Empower the Church to be transformed into the image of Jesus Christ. Release Your power to bring healing to the sick, freedom to the possessed, comfort to those who mourn and release for those who are oppressed. Come and melt the hearts of people to love again. Enfold the weak, the orphans, the widows and elderly in Your arms. Please answer the call of the homeless, the hungry, the helpless and the dying. Display Your mercy and provide for our needs. Give us wisdom and insight in every sphere of life that we will find the answers to the needs of the world. Help us to use the resources of the earth for the well-being of all. Pour Your love into our hearts and fill us with compassion and let the power of the Holy Spirit characterize our lives.

Holy Spirit, we need Your comfort and guidance. Come and transform our lives.

Lord, Jesus Christ, You were dead, but are now risen. Because the Father has given You a Name above all names, You will defeat all powers of evil. You have declared that the gates of hell will not prevail against

ENCOURAGE

Your Church. We pray for deliverance from demonic oppression. We pray for the tearing down of the strongholds and ideologies that hinder and resist the spreading of the knowledge of God. We resist the plan of the enemy to keep nations in darkness and pray that You will remove the veil that covers the peoples. We ask for open doors so that the gospel can enter into every nation. Restrain the evil that promotes violence and death. Break the hold of slavery and tyranny. Fill us with courage to fearlessly and faithfully preach Your Word. Give us a spirit of intercession to cry on behalf of the lost.

Almighty God, deliver us from evil and the Evil One.

King of Glory, we invite You to come to the nations of the world. God has promised long ago that You would come to restore all things. We welcome You to finish Your work in our cities, our peoples and our nations. Together we cry, "Lift up your heads, O you gates. Be lifted up ancient doors, so that the King of Glory may enter in." King of Kings, You will be exalted among the nations of the earth. We now join our hearts with all the believers across the whole world, from Africa, from the Middle East, from North and South America, from Asia, from Europe, from Australia and from the Pacific Islands. We lift up our voices together in unison:

The Spirit and the Bride say: "Come Lord Jesus."

Something to think about before you close this book today:

Look again through this prayer and underline several of the requests that are what your heart is saying.

ENCOURAGE

For This I Need Jesus

Each Wednesday morning at 6:30 I meet with thirty or forty men and women in what we call "The Dead Theologian's Society". You can guess what we do: read books by dead theologians. One time the leader asked us if anyone knew what the first thesis was of Luther's "Ninety-five Thesis." None of us could answer. Our leader then quoted Luther.

When our Lord and Master Jesus Christ said, "Repent" (Mt 4:17), he willed the entire life of believers to be one of repentance.

My first thought: That's profound! My second: What in the world does that really mean? That morning I heard a great illustration of what it meant when one of the members, Bill, wondered aloud: "What goes on in my life as I try to follow Christ?" He continued. "Let me tell you of an incident that happened just yesterday. I was driving on the interstate in Chattanooga, keeping to the speed limit. I saw a car on the highway in front of me, going very slowly, almost at a standstill. I glided to the middle lane. Then someone behind me, apparently going quite a bit faster than the speed limit, blew his horn and kept blaring it.

"My anger immediately exploded. I wanted to punch that horn blowing guy in the nose." (Everyone at the meeting chuckled, but our excited story teller continued on.) "That crazy driver should have seen the car in front of me. He saw that I had to pull over. Why was he going so fast anyway? He didn't need to honk his horn so long. My anger grew! It kept boiling inside." Bill continued after he paused to calm down.

"After so many years when I have grown so much in following Christ, why is this explosive temper, that part of my old man, still so strong in me?"

Our leader mentioned something he had heard from a friend who had experienced something similar. The friend said: "For this, I need Jesus."

ENCOURAGE

And then smilingly he said to Bill, "Maybe you need to put that on your dashboard." We all laughed.

And I thought, "I may need to put that on my dashboard." For I realized the quote was a perfect illustration of what Luther's first thesis meant. I need Jesus' forgiveness for my entire life. Many times a day I need to repent of a thought or an action and receive the forgiveness God is offering, as do we all. There are so many times each day when I should look at what is going on in me or around me and say to myself, "For that, I need Jesus."

Bill had just finished his story when a young woman told of something she had recently experienced. She had been quite offended and with Christ's help fought through what the old nature was raising within her. An older friend of hers said to her, "Jesus just got a little sweeter, didn't he? "

Putting all that together I realized how encouraging all that was for me. I hope that is encouraging for you too. When we experience an offense, or face a tough situation, and, in our response blow it as a Christian, that needs not be the discouraging end of it. For Jesus "willed the entire life of believers to be one of repentance."

Of course, that's true. So many times a day I repent of what I was thinking or saying or doing. And there is always--and immediately--forgiveness. And the reminder that "Jesus just got a little sweeter" is another gracious reminder that "for this, I need Jesus."

Put that little phrase on your dashboard or your refrigerator door... or in your heart—

Talk to someone today about a time when you put into practice Luther's first thesis and how, "Jesus just got a little sweeter."

Grow Where You Are Planted

As a member of a serious discussion group with the humorous name, "The Dead Theologians' Society," we had the assignment to read, *The Rare Jewel of Christian Contentment,* by Jeremiah Burroughs, an English Puritan pastor who lived and wrote in the mid 1600's. Our discussion brought out a number of ideas that encouraged me as I have sought to live for Christ. Perhaps my thoughts will help you in your walk with Him..

Once a friend in a nursing home, limited to her bed, was asked how she was doing. "I am happy in Jesus," was her reply. And she was. No word of anxiety, complaint or worry. When anyone visited her they would leave feeling blessed.

How did she learn to live like that?

She looked beyond the affliction. She was not problem centered, rather God centered. Some ask, "Why me?" She affirmed, "Here is my opportunity to grow, to draw closer to God."

As we students of *Dead Theologians* discussed the "why me" equation with one another, one lawyer said, "I think we are called to grow where we are planted. God knows that some of us will do well in the sun and some in the shade and some will grow like mushrooms, producing even more when planted in dung." We all laughed, but we realized that some in our group had experienced an easy life; others had gone through deep waters, learning that only when they trusted in our sovereign and loving God would they have contentment in those difficult situations that He allows. One in the group added, "We think we have to understand what God is doing in order to love and follow him. But when we can't understand Him, He is still to be loved and obeyed. Think of pioneer missionaries like Adonirum Judson or William Carey. They had very few converts during their ministries. They never saw the wave of God followers that resulted from their faithful testimonies. But now *we* can."

A pastor in our serious and thoughtful group admitted, "I'm a heat seeking missile of worry. I solve one thing I am worried about and...beep, beep, beep...I start looking for something else to worry about." That pastor is one of the godliest persons I know, but he knows himself very well and is honest enough to admit he is far from maturity in Christ. Even the Apostle Paul, early in his Christian life called himself the "least of the apostles," (lowest of thirteen). A few years later he called himself the least Christian, (the worst Christian among hundreds). Close to the end of his life he called himself "the chief of sinners," (the worst among thousands). As someone said, "The closer one gets to the light, the darker the shadows become."

As we each mature in Christ in our individual ways, we see ourselves more clearly and realize what sins remain to be dealt with. Actually that is good not bad.

What can keep us from getting discouraged and giving up? Someone in our group wisely said, "We must acknowledge our sin and fallenness and, more than that, acknowledge God's love and forgiveness. Receiving and holding on to *the truth of imputed righteousness* is the only way." We are not God's child because of how well we live, but because of the truth of John 1:12. "Yet to all who received him, to those who believed in his name, he gave the right to become children of God." We are adopted. We are loved. The penalty for our sins has been paid in full by Christ and we are forgiven!

As Gert Behanna, who wrote *The Late Liz*, said, "I am not what I want to be. I am not what I am going to be, but, praise God; I am not what I used to be."

Be encouraged.

A question to think about before you close this book today:

What is going on in your life now that you don't like or don't understand? How can it become an opportunity to draw closer to God?

How to Keep Close to the Lord

I have been reading a delightful book: *Select Letters of John Newton*. One of the letters is his response to a lady who asked him, "What are the best means to prevent the world from drawing one's heart aside from God?"

I love his response and thought you might find it as encouraging and challenging as I did.

Newton first pointed out in his reply that from her question he discerned that in her heart she probably already knew what he would say-- because it would come from the Bible, which she knew as well as he did. But then he admitted, "If your heart is like mine, I must confess, that when I turn aside from God, it is seldom though ignorance of the proper means which should have kept us near him, but rather from an evil principal within us." Newton wrote that the real question was: "How does one effectively reduce the impact of this evil principle?

Newton pointed out that though it is one's duty and privilege to keep close to the Lord, we must not expect to do this perfectly or at once. That is a good thought for us who often feel guilty about our not keeping our eyes on God. Newton added that we can keep close to Him the more we see clearly the infinite disparity between God and the little things that draw our attention from him and recognize the folly of giving them our time and interest. But we only learn these things by experience and failings. How often have I said that living for God is better than life, then, a mere trifle turns my focus from God and I am embroiled in worry, fear or ugly thoughts.

Newton said something we don't often hear from the pulpit. "God permits us to feel our weakness so that we might more quickly be alert to it." We often say that we know we are weak creatures, yet we don't really know the depth of this until God allows us to face a trial and fall. We fall because we are depending on some strength within and only then do we truly understand how desperately we need to stay close to God.

Newton summarizes his thought. "The only sure secret of walking closely with God is to be humble like a little child who is so very conscience of the dangers around it that it is afraid of taking a step alone, therefore it cries out continually for its father or mother to stay close that it may be safe.

That makes sense to me, but then I wonder: how does one attain that *humble spirit*? In a way it is like the man who told his apprentice that the key to success was to make right decisions. The apprentice asked, "How do I learn to make the right decisions?" "By making bad decisions."

Newton said we learn humility when we gain a clear conviction of our weaknesses and sinfulness. And we don't learn that from books or sermons. In God's wisdom, he allows us to see ourselves as we truly are. And it is often not a very pretty picture. Thankfully, most of us, by God's mercy, have not gotten so involved with the world that those around us have recognized the depth of our fallenness. But we know that as others look at us, judging only by our outward actions, they may see nothing of great sinfulness. But we know they are not seeing our thoughts and the first motions of our heart. How devastating it would be for all our thoughts to be immediately put on our timeline on Facebook. I imagine that would help keep us humble and very aware of our weaknesses.

So, what are we to do? Our often failings should keep us aware of how weak we are. But we forget so quickly. Can we do anything to help us maintain a humble spirit and keep alert to our weakness, so we don't so often fall? Newton told the lady he was writing to that she already knew what to do. But then he repeated it. He first mentioned prayer. He said she should simply pray for humility. I haven't done that very often.

He said she should stay involved with the Word. Psalm 119:9, 11 clearly points this out. "How can a young man keep his way pure? By guarding it according to your word. Your word have I hidden in my heart, that I might not sin against you." He pointed out that in the Bible we discover the *precepts* that guide us on a good path. We find the *promises* that give us strength and encouragement. We read of the lives of God's saints. Their *failings are signposts* set to guide us around the mud holes and pits on our journey. The *good recorded* about their lives brings us encouragement. He said that as we meditate on the whole scheme of the good news, the record of Jesus' person, life, teaching, death, and glory, it

ENCOURAGE

gradually molds our souls in such a way that we slowly begin to recognize "the trifles that would draw us from God." They lose their influence and we begin to see them for what they are. Their glitter is seen to be just vanity and nothing.

Newton's third means of "staying close to the Lord" is so obvious I should have thought of it, but I hadn't. It is consideration or recollection. We need to be alert to those temptations and snares that, because of our personalities or temperaments, we more easily fall to.

For example, our daughter-in-law is allergic to bee stings. So she tries to be alert to the presence of bees. Likewise, I've often stumbled into very bad cases of poison ivy. This week on a delightful hike I was constantly looking out for those three-leafed bad guys. Happily, nothing. Newton said that it would be wise if "in the morning, ere we leave our chambers, to forecast, as far as we are able, the probable circumstances of the day before us." What does it look like that we will be facing today that often causes us to stumble?

Newton's last sentence to his inquiring lady is an encouragement to us also. "However, I trust the Lord, who has given you a desire to live to him, will be your guard and teacher. There is none teacheth like him."

I feel sure that you, like Newton's lady, want to "prevent the world, with all its opening and ensnaring scenes, from drawing the heart aside from God." Hopefully, these thought from John Newton have been a challenge, but also an encouragement.

<u>Select Letters of John Newton</u>, The Banner of Truth Trust, pp. 200-202.

Something to do today: The lady asked Newton, "What are the best means to prevent the world from drawing one's heart aside from God?" Newton recommended: "humble prayer for God's help, involvement with God's work and recollection, being alert to what causes us to fall." Discuss this with someone today and share with them what you especially need to work on. Write here someone you think you could do this with.

_____

Hungering and Thirsting

Blessed are those who hunger and thirst for righteousness for they will be filled. Matt 5:6

I want to be blessed; I want to be filled with righteousness, Christ righteousness and righteous living. Jesus was the one who said that if I hungered and thirsted for righteousness I *would be* blessed and filled. What does that mean? What is the righteousness we are to seek? What does it mean to *hunger* and *thirst* after it?

In the Bible *righteousness* include includes a right relationship with God and with others. So the desire for righteousness, includes both justification, and sanctification--the desire to be free of the entanglements of sin in all their seductive forms.

I'm sure that that is what we all want, the desire to be holy, to display the beatitudes in our daily life, to experience the fruit of the Spirit in all we do, actually, to be like Jesus.

What is it like to hunger and thirst? We've all experienced those moments of thirst, starting with our infant whimperings that soon lead to howls for mother's milk or later with curses during those unending military treks when our canteens were dry.

I've not really known much abject hunger or *desperate* thirst. Oh, perhaps, after working a full day in in the sun doing yard work, or playing summer basketball with the guys to the point of exhaustion. I was really thirsty, not just a passing thirst, but water, now!

"As the deer pants for streams of water, so I long for you, O God. My soul thirsts for...the living God" (Psalm 42:1). That's the thirst Jesus was talking about.

ENCOURAGE

I remember a time when I felt spiritually dry, thirsty. It was my second year in college. I was not the person I knew that God wanted me to be. I tried to be better but usually failed even living up to my own standards. But when the Good News of what Christ had done for me was presented in the most lively and refreshing way, I could do nothing but drink deeply and be refreshed in my heart and life. I was justified. The barriers of sin and guilt between God and me were removed. My hunger and thirst were satisfied. And it happened immediately.

Fairly quickly, however, I was confronted with the reality that I was not done with the dryness of sin. At times I'd choose what I knew was wrong. But God's Spirit did not leave me, thus I began to desire what pleased Him. There grew over time a curious hunger and thirst for developing Christ likeness. To be sure, sometimes I was not always strong or wise. I'd choose sin; often I was selfish and realized I wasn't always hungry or thirsty to be freed from those titillating, nagging sins.

Happily, over the years God worked in my life and slowly conformed me more to His image. My hungering and thirsting for righteousness, for justice, for right living with others, became stronger.

I had hungered for and received the righteousness of Christ that brought me salvation, justification. I was now hungering for sanctification, Christlikeness. It didn't take me long to recognize that I could not obtain that by myself but I could refrain from doing those things that were obviously opposed to a Christ likeness. As Lloyd-Jones wrote in his book: *Sermon on the Mount*, "I can never make myself like Jesus Christ, but I can stop walking in the gutters of life." (pg.90). If there is an infection in a house, avoid that house.

I can (if I'm not a physician or a fumigator) try to avoid things that are wrong or harmful for me or others, and also try to avoid things that dull my spiritual appetites. There are perfectly legitimate things that are harmless in themselves, but when I spend too much time with them (has anyone heard of TV or Facebook), I desire the things of God less. Similarly, I dull my healthy appetite by eating too much junk food. There is something like that in the spiritual realm.

ENCOURAGE

Consequently, I am called to discipline myself to keep before me my need to hunger and thirst for righteousness. So often when I get super busy it takes discipline to remind myself of my need for righteousness. Living the Christian life does take discipline. It doesn't come naturally. And while thinking about that I have to remember that blessed are those who recognize their spiritual poverty. I need to ask for God's help to even want to discipline myself in this way.

But when I ask for God's help and take the effort to hunger and thirst for righteousness, God always rewards my efforts--often in surprising ways. Do you remember blind Bartimaeus, the man described in Mark's eleventh chapter? Poor, bedraggled Bartimaeus could not heal his own blindness for there were no ointments or ophthalmologists then, but he put himself in front of Jesus who could and did heal him. I can put myself before Jesus.

The world, the flesh and the devil hit us all the time, thus we cannot afford to lose any opportunity to put our self where we can learn and receive righteousness. Worship, prayer, solitude, the sacraments, fellowship, reading and meditating on the Bible, reading Christian biographies are the things that put us in front of Jesus.

When one joins the church I am a member of, one of the questions they must answer is: I promise to make diligent use of the means of grace. The things I just mentioned are some of the "means of grace". Make diligent use of them. You'll find yourself more and more hungering and thirsting for righteousness.

A question to think about before you close the book today:

Which "means of grace" do you find most puts you in front of Jesus? Consider doing it more.

ENCOURAGE

Is It All Up to You?

Have you ever taught a class or lead a discussion and wondered if you had done a good job? Had I asked the right questions? Did the students understand the material? Were they now able to go into the world and live better for the Lord?

Those are not bad questions; but be careful about thinking that your students' abilities to become leaders, to mature in Christ, to witness and lead others to him is dependent on how well we led the class and how well we have discipled them. If a person truly has Christ in his or her life, they can serve the Lord well from their first days as a follower of Jesus. Discipleship training can be very helpful in the maturing process of young Christians, but each is sealed in the Holy Spirit, has immediate and constant access to God, and has the power of the Scriptures available.

I've been reading a good book, *Organic Church*. The author, Neil Cole, points out that the only spiritual difference between a new Christian and one who has walked with God for years, is maturity. The spiritual empowerment is the same. Maturity makes a difference, but that maturing is gained through experiences, not just in a classroom.

Jesus said to the disciples "The harvest is plentiful, but the workers are few. Ask the Lord of the harvest, therefore, to send out workers into his harvest field." Where did he expect the workers to come from? Not a band of angels, surely, not just the twelve who had been with him. The workers for his harvest must come from the recently harvested. Converts were to be the workers. Cole wrote, "We have made a terrible mistake by separating the convert from the worker. They are not two but one. Each new convert is a new worker. We are remiss when we expect the convert to wait a while, *any time at all*, to become a worker. Each new convert is a worker immediately."

ENCOURAGE

I have seen, and feel sure you have too, new Christians lead friends and relatives to Christ. There was the Ethiopian eunuch. God sent him back with only part of the Old Testament in his hand and the Holy Spirit in his heart. If God could trust him to be a worker in the field, not having much discipleship training, we can trust that others can serve the Lord well even while studying and maturing in Christ. One doesn't have to wait for greater maturity before he or she can serve the Lord. And it is not all our responsibility to teach and lead Christians toward maturity so that they can finally (phew) work for God. God has already given them what they need to serve him.

It is encouraging to me to remember that people's conversions are not all up to me. I have been called to teach and lead, but each believer already has what they need to begin to be an instrument in God's hands. I must not underestimate what God can do through a new believer or a growing one who desires to follow Christ. Nor should I think that all the weight is on my shoulders to train some new potential leader to become a mature follower of Christ. Sure we have a job to do and we are called to do it well. But happily it is God who causes the growth. *So neither he who plants nor he who waters is anything, but only God who makes things grow (I Cor. 3:7).* I hope that is also encouraging to you.

A question to ask yourself before you close this book today:

What younger/newer believer are you in contact with whom you can encourage with these thoughts?

I'll try to contact _____ *this week.*

Keep Plugged In

I can really know Christ and experience the mighty power that raised him from the dead. I can learn what it means to suffer with him, sharing in his death, so that somehow, I can experience the resurrection from the dead!

Philippians 3:10, 11

In Philippians, Paul wrote of wanting to experience *the power of Jesus' resurrection.*

As I reread those verses I was led to think about the power that we need to live all that Christ Jesus saves us for and wants us to be. None of us can just coast through life, especially if we want to live for God--for that takes energy, effort, and stamina.

I thought about two kinds of power: power to control things and energy to get through things. Someone wrote, "Your personal power probably peaked the first month of your life. At that point the entire world revolved around you and you weren't even fully aware of it. But any time you made just a little whimper, all these big adults rallied to your attention. You were fed, burped, changed, cuddled and rocked. You were given attention. And in your little infantile mind you figured out, 'This works! When I cry I get attention.' That's called power."

However, we all discovered that, as we grew up, two awful things happened. 1) The world became difficult and complicated, and 2), people stopped paying attention to our whimpering. Part of growing up is realizing how much of our life is really out of our control. When we're young, we think we can control about everything. Remember that *great theologian*, the film actor, Leonardo DiCaprio, who said in the block buster film, "Titanic", "I am the king of the world!"

However, much of all of our lives is out of our control, yet it is human nature for us to try to control the uncontrollable. Unfortunately, we get tired, emotionally distraught, physically fatigued and spiritually defeated. We soon discover that we are not created to handle this world on our own. This is because God has built us to have a relationship with Him as we move through life.

Conversely, we can discover and know Jesus as the one who has all the power we need and is eager to share his power. He heals the sick, calms the storms, brings himself back to life with his power over death. The Bible teaches that, *as we are united to Christ*, his resurrection power is available to us as well.

What kind of power does Jesus Christ offer us? He offers us power to change our life, the power to change the unchangeable, those things we'd like to change about ourselves and have tried to change, but can't: habits, hang-ups, hurts that keep messing up our life. He gives us the power to let go of guilt, to let go of grief. He gives us the power to let go of the grudges that keep us stuck in the past and keep us from getting on with life. He gives us the power to forgive ourselves and to forgive others. He gives us the power to start over when we've really made a mess of life and we feel like we've failed. He gives us the power to keep going when we're discouraged and think we can't take another step. He gives us the power to become what we were always meant to be in the first place. His resurrection power is available to us as well.

Do you remember these promises from the Bible? *"I can do everything God asks me to do with the help of Christ who strengthens me with power." "God will strengthen you with his own great power so that you will not give up when trouble comes."* He not only gives us starting power but also staying power. *"God never grows faint or weary. He gives power to those who are tired and worn out. Those who wait on the Lord will find new strength. They will fly high on wings like eagles!"*

ENCOURAGE

If you are tired, get plugged into the source of energizing power--and get some rest. For you might have become tired because you've been trying to handle life on your own or just plugging into the source of power *now and then*. I read about a survey that showed that a high percentage of pastors of large churches, because of their exhausting routines, do not have a daily, meaningful time with God by reading his word and in meditating prayer.

We have a small handheld vacuum cleaner called a *Dust Buster*. I unplug it and start using it to vacuum. It does what it is built to do. You can even set it down and use it the next day. It will still pick up some light dirt. Set it down again and the next day it will still work but not as well. Soon it will be out of power and won't function. That's because it had not been recharged from its source of power. We, as well, need to stay *plugged into* Jesus, our source of power.

He waits to empower you with Himself. Don't neglect your time with him because your life has been busy. We shouldn't neglect our only true source of power that enables us to move well through life. Resurrection power *is* available to us.

A question to ask yourself before you close this book today:

What keeps you from staying plugged into Christ? What can/will you do about that?

ENCOURAGE

My Job Isn't to Produce

Oh, Word of God
produce in me
a bud ,,, a flower ... who knows
a tree
a gentle shade for those in need,
a place where hungry ones can feed
a watered garden I would be ...
oh, Word of God
rain down on me.
            Jill Briscoe "Heartbeat"

Is not that your desire too? I have no doubt that it is or you would not be reading this "Encourage." When I read Jill's poem I noticed a subtle, but important, thought included in it. Her prayer isn't "Make me a tree," but "produce in me..." What is the difference?

I have recently been thinking of John 15 and fruit in the Christian life. I certainly don't want to be a barren tree. I want to have much fruit in my life. I'm sure you do too. What Jesus' words in John 15 have shown me is that I really don't produce the fruit. My job is not to produce fruit, but to "abide" in Jesus. It doesn't say: go to church, tithe, live a disciplined life, keep the Sabbath, witness to people, teach the Bible, rededicate your life, feed the poor, try to live like Jesus did and you'll produce fruit. It simply says for us to "abide" and then ... "abide." "Whoever abides in me and I in him, he it is that bears much fruit" (John 15:5). It is the inevitable result of abiding in Jesus to see fruit produced in our lives. The fruit of the Spirit (Christ likeness): "love joy, peace, patience, kindness, goodness,

ENCOURAGE

faithfulness, gentleness and self-control" are produced by the Spirit of God as we abide in Jesus. In Galatians 5 Paul contrasted the "fruit of the Spirit" with the "works of the flesh." Notice that Paul doesn't say the "weeds of the flesh." Why the mixed metaphor? Because the "works of the flesh" are what we do. The "fruit of the Spirit" is what God produces through us as we abide in Jesus.

Isn't that wonderful? God doesn't command us to rededicate our lives and work hard to be like Jesus. Be like Jesus! We can't be like Michael Jordan, Payton Manning or Steph Curry! And trying harder won't make it no matter how much time we have or how hard we try. We are not called to work our tail off to serve God by teaching, ministering to people and living a strong Christian life and that will mean a fruitful life. Our job is to "abide" and then ... "to abide."

What exactly does it mean to abide? We get a clue from John 15:7. "If you abide in me, and my words abide in you..." Oh, dear friend, let the Word of God abide, live, dwell, remain in you and you will produce much fruit. Do that and it is inevitable. It is a process. It will take time. Fruit on a tree doesn't appear in a day. But if the branches are abiding in the trunk, the apples will come.

I have a friend who had a fiery temper and a dirty mouth. He came to faith in Christ and over the years, his temper came out less and less. Recently I was with him and I saw that old nature come out several times. I asked him how his time with the Lord was going. He said he had been regular in God's Word, but in recent months it has been almost nothing. What had happened? He was not "abiding" in Jesus. He was not letting God's Word abide in him, and the fruit of kindness, gentleness and self-control were no longer being produced through him.

How can all this be encouraging to us? Because we are not called to do something we can't do like: Follow Jesus example; stop being so angry, etc. What we are called to do, we can do. It is not easy, but we can do it. Abide in Christ and let his Word abide in us ... and we will produce much fruit. We will be transformed from within by the renewal of our mind, Romans 12:2. We will know God's will, realize that it is right and will delight in doing it.

Be encouraged.

ENCOURAGE

A question to ask yourself before you close this book today: You are a branch. How are you doing abiding in the vine? Take a minute to think about how you can improve the connection? Write it down here.

_____

ENCOURAGE

Our Eternal Tender

I just read the book, *Tender Care*, written by the Barnabas staff. In it I discovered there are great parallels to what missionaries face and what a commercial, hard hat diver faces.

In one of my first jobs as a commercial diver in the Everglades of Southern Florida, I was in a canal, in water so murky I couldn't see six inches in front of me. My tender (the one on shore guiding me and assuring that I have the right air) pointed out the general direction of the job site below. He helped me suit up, handed me my tools, and pointed across the black water toward the job site.

As a young, confident diver, I was sure I could find and do the job in complete darkness. I had not yet come to value advice from my tender, nor was I accustomed to hearing his voice in my helmet radio.

I entered a black new world toward the job site. Several times I overshot the prescribed location. I could not find it! What I had not yet learned was that once I was in complete darkness, without a fixed point of reference, disorientation took over.

My tender kept calling me on the radio, trying to direct my steps. He could see my air bubbles crisscrossing the canal as I wandered all over the bottom in search of the job site. I finally paused long enough to hear him, he took a bearing on my location and confidently and professionally gave me clear directions.

Not only did my tender help me get to the job site, but he kept watch for certain dangers of which I was unaware. While I worked in the dark below, my tender had spotted a nine-foot alligator lurking on the surface. He knew not alert me until there was a threat. And even then, he simply said I needed to return to the surface...now! He removed my heavy, awkward helmet and pointed to the angry danger lurking nearby.

ENCOURAGE

The eyes of the tender were crucial to my success in accomplishing the job. He knew the dangers beyond my ability to see and watched on my behalf for such threats.

We too have a tender, an Eternal Tender. And God in His wisdom sends us to job sites with significant, sometimes frightening tasks for us to do. He guides us with tender care. Like the diver, it is important to make sure that we are intently listening for our Tender's guidance.

I am certain I have headed out to do a job God has given me to do and I have neglected to keep in touch with Him. Sure, I have ended up being surprised, angry and disoriented. But God was always watching my *air bubbles* and knew I was just wandering around without a fixed point of reference. Sure, He called to me, but often I was so busy trying to do it all myself, I didn't hear His voice. Happily, I finally paused long enough to hear him. He always knows exactly what needs to be done at a given time and place and will assure us of the right path.

How encouraging to know that our Tender never gets distracted. His eyes are always on us, guiding and protecting us. Our job? Carefully keeping alert to our Tender's wise and loving voice and following his instructions.

Tender Care, **Barnabas Books**, Rockford, IL, 2010, pg. 11.

Something to think about before you close this book today:

Take a minute or two and think of a time when God was your Eternal Tender. Thank him.

ENCOURAGE

Plus Ultra

Recently, I was reading Randy Alcorn's excellent book, Heaven, when two Latin words of his text caught my attention: *plus ultra*.

In high school, unfortunately, I took woodworking instead of Latin. Consequently, I've always felt a bit intimidated by italicized words in so many books that are calculated to impress readers, or are the authors hope that readers will be impressed by their erudition. So when an author translates Latin words, I pay particular attention and try to learn some of what I missed in high school.

Plus Ultra, Alcorn wrote means *more beyond*. (You probably already knew that.) He explained that after Columbus discovered the new world, Spain minted coins with this Latin slogan on them. It was a horizon-expanding message to people who'd believed that their world was all there was.

Alcorn wrote, "*Plus Ultra*--there will always be more to discover about our God."

I now try to keep that thought in the front of my mind. Most of you, I suspect, who read this "Encourage", have been followers of Christ for many years. But as time goes by, being the frail human beings we are, it is easy to take for granted our relationship with God, to let our time with him become stale and our ministry for him to lose its fervency. When I read a familiar Psalm or a chapter of a Gospel, the thought sneakily passes through my aging brain that there wasn't much new in that passage. Likewise, when I am preparing to lead a Bible study it can more mechanical rather than freshly exciting. The temptation is to be satisfied, though a bit disappointed, with what then becomes inevitable, dullness in our walk with Christ.

So, we need to remember *Plus Ultra*, "more beyond." There is always more to discover about God and his work in our lives and ministry. We need to remember what the senior demon, *Screwtape*, in C. S. Lewis'

ENCOURAGE

Screwtape Letters, says to his junior tempter, *Wormwood*. Humans are "amphibians, half spirit, and half animal." Then Screwtape educates Wormwood. "Their nearest approach to constancy, therefore, is undulation—the repeated return to a level from which they repeatedly fall back, a series of troughs and peaks." He goes on, "The dryness and dullness through which your patient is now going are not, as you fondly suppose, *your* workmanship; they are merely a natural phenomenon which will do us no good unless you make a good use of it." Screwtape adds, "It is during such trough periods, much more than during the peak periods, that it (a Christian) is growing into the sort of creature He (God) wants it to be. Hence the prayers offered in the state of dryness are those which please Him best."

So be encouraged. Whenever you go through a time of dryness and dullness in your devotions or ministry, you are experiencing the effects of being a son or daughter of Adam, an *amphibian*, half spirit/half animal. Such feelings happen to the most godly men and women.

But don't then just relax and do nothing. Move ahead; make diligent use of the means of grace: prayer, Bible meditation, worship, the sacraments, fellowship, etc. Oswald Chambers wrote, "When it comes to taking the initiative against drudgery, we have to take the first step. There is no point in waiting for God to help us—He will not. But once we arise, immediately we find He is there."

Therefore, we are called, as a former President of Wheaton College often reminded the gathered students, to "keep on keeping on."

Something to think about before you close this book today:

If you are now or when you come to a time of spiritual dryness, what are the first steps you would take to move ahead?

Also remind yourself that God is much greater in every way than we can even comprehend. Ultra plus, there is "more beyond" to discover about God and what he has for you to do.

Take Time to Smell the Roses

I recently read of something interesting that took place in a Washington, D.C. subway station. On a cold January morning in 2007, a commonplace, middle-aged man stood playing a violin as hundreds of people walked by, most hurrying on their way to work.

After he had played for about four minutes, a woman threw a crumpled dollar into the man's violin case, and continued walking, barely slowing down. A young man paused for a moment, looked at his watch, then headed off.

At the 45-minute mark, six people had stopped and listened, each for only for a moment. Some dropped a few coins as they quickly walked on. Exactly $32 had landed in the open violin case.

After an hour, the man stopped playing, packed up his violin and left. No one noticed.

The violinist no one recognized was the renowned Joshua Bell, one of the greatest musicians in the world. He had played several magnificent Bach etudes in that subway station, on a Stradivarius valued at $3.5 million. A couple of days earlier, in Boston, Bell had played the same music to a packed theater. Tickets averaged $100 a seat.

The train station event was organized by The Washington Post as part of a social experiment about people's perceptions, tastes and priorities. The experiment ended with several interesting questions.

In a common-place environment, at an inappropriate hour, do we perceive beauty? Do we stop to appreciate it? Do we recognize talent in an unexpected context?

ENCOURAGE

My busy friend, would you have walked right past that musician or would you have stopped and listened? I think I probably would have rushed on, thinking, "I have to get to work. I've a lot of important things to do."

If we unthinkingly do not take a moment to stop and listen to one of the most gifted musicians in the world, playing some of the finest music ever written, on one of the most beautiful instruments ever made, how many other things might we be missing as we rush through life? Probably, many more than we realize. But it's worthwhile to stay alert to the glories of the world around us and not live so that we are always rushed.

Though this is a fallen world, it is still a world created by the Master Designer. There are beauties all around, often beyond description. Many are seen in nature, others in the arts, but the most wondrous are those to whom God has called us to minister. What a privilege we have every day to encounter and rub shoulders with God's chosen people.

As C.S. Lewis wrote, "...remember that the dullest and most uninteresting person you talk to may one day be a creature which, if you saw it now, you would be strongly tempted to worship ... There are no ordinary people. You have never talked to a mere mortal. Nations, cultures, arts, civilization—these are mortal ... But it is immortals whom we joke with, marry, snub, and exploit..." C. S. Lewis (The Weight of Glory, p.15).

Think of it. There are glories all around you. Some of them even live in your house with you.

So enjoy them NOW.

Something to do before you close this book today:

Read C.S. Lewis' quote again and plan on how you might deal differently today with one of those seemingly "ordinary people" God brings into your life.

ENCOURAGE

The Duck Tape Wallet

It was the second annual family camp we put on for the Iraqi believers in northern Iraq. The camp is the one time a year when 150-200 Iraqi believers can get together for fellowship, worship and teaching...and fun. The adults would be getting some good biblical teaching in the mornings. The teens would have some time together for games and Bible teaching. During the same time, we had something like Vacation Bible School for the children.

But what would we do during the afternoons? There needed to be some time for rest, some time for the people to just hang out together and talk with friends they only get to see once or twice a year. Then someone came up with the idea of having a variety of crafts for people do. This would help build relationships as people did things together. It could be fun, relaxing and still create something useful.

Ideas were thrown out. For adults and teens we came up with making ear rings and picture frames for photos we would take of each family. Then the idea was presented of making duct tape wallets. I volunteered for this. I like doing things with my hands. When I went to our local Hobby Lobby store, I discovered that duct tape is not what the wallets should be made of.

Duct tape is a thick, strong, very sticky silver backed tape used to tape air and heating ducts together. The craft that has come out of this now uses Duck Tape (not duct tape). Duck Tape is thinner and less sticky. (But I and everyone who worked with it discovered it is still sticky.) Duck Tape is not just silver or black like duct tape, but every color you can think of plus camouflage, leopard skin, polka dot, flame and more. So I made Hobby Lobby a bit richer and bought some of almost color and pattern.

I then went to You Tube and found an instruction clip of a teenager putting together a very nice Duck Tape wallet. I quickly decided, "That will be the pattern." I watched the You Tube presentation many times and took detailed notes: height, width, size of pockets, etc. I made several with different colored tape, each one looking a bit more like a wallet. Then I thought about the Iraqi money I had from a previous trip. Are those bills the same size as the dollar? Opps...no! The smaller the currency amount, the smaller the bill. The larger the currency amount, the larger the bill and one of the most used bill is quite a bit larger than the American dollar. So back to square one with the measurements. Finally, after several failed attempts the perfect dimensions were determined.

When I and my box of multicolored duck tapes made it to Iraq and the family camp and people came to make their wallets, I discovered something. Not only adult men and older teenagers wanted to make themselves a wallet, but young teens and even younger girls wanted to also. The razor sharp exacto knives I brought to cut the tape patterns would be lethal weapons in a twelve-year old's hands. That led to increased prayer and more training for the two leaders I had trained to help people make the wallets.

So people started on their wallets. The adults picked classic, attractive looking colors: brown and black. The teenaged boys choose zebra or flame tape. The girls choose not one color but usually two or three very bright colors, not always exactly blending together according to the color chart. The eleven-year-old boys went for the camouflage tape. The young girls liked pink and yellow. Prayers were answered in that no one cut their finger. A lot of tape was wasted as one piece of the pattern became stuck to another that were not to be together. Duck Tape is still sticky. But dozens of wallets were completed that week. One wife came in and asked if I would help her make one for her husband. She was so careful in cutting the tape and putting the pieces together. It probably turned out to be the best looking one of them all...except for one.

A twelve-year-old girl carefully worked on hers for two afternoons. She picked out two nice colors that blended well together. She finished the wallet and it looked good. Then she took a piece of pink tape and started cutting out something. I thought, "Not pink! That doesn't blend with other colors. The wallet is finished. It already looks great. What is she doing? She'll mess it up." I thought she made an aesthetic mistake, but I was wrong. It was beautiful. This young girl living in a Muslim world had cut out a pink cross and placed on the middle of her wallet for all to see.

ENCOURAGE

I am a pretty organized person. If the napkins on the table are crooked, without thinking I straighten them. I basically know what colors match and what patterns don't. The piles of books and papers on my desk are straight piles. I believe my wife thinks that there shouldn't be piles of papers and books on my desk, but at least mine are neat piles.

When I saw the young girl putting something pink on her (to my mind) completed, color coordinated wallet, I immediately thought she was doing the wrong thing. It didn't fit what I thought of as "the way things should be" or "the right way to do things." Oh, where are my priorities? What is really important? It is not "doing things the *right* way," which too often just happens to be *my* way.

I was reminded that I am to "do nothing out of vain conceit, but in humility consider others better that myself…and…look not only to my own interests, but also to the interests of others" (Philippians 4:3-4). "Do not think of yourself more highly than you ought" (Romans 12:3). I now think more highly of a twelve-year-old Iraqi girl's decision on how to decorate her Duck Tape wallet than I do of my carefully color coordinated choices.

Thank you, Lord. I need a bit more…a lot more… humility.

If you do too, be encouraged. If you are praying for more humility, I really believe God will answer your prayer.

Something to think about before you close this book today:

What is one of your "right way of doing things" and when someone does it differently it "gets to you"? Is your way the right way or just another way of doing it?

The Power of Poetry

I never really appreciated poetry. That's probably why in college I majored in mathematics and minored in physics and in the navy became an engineering officer. I could even proudly recite the arithmetic *pi* to the 10th digit. Okay, it's 3.141592653589793.

Once in a high school Lit. Class, I was required to read some famous poem (oh, probably an obscure Shakespearian sonnet or other), but I had no clue what Sir William was saying. I probably even fell asleep before finishing that long piece of pentameter verse.

However, there was one lovely poem that caught my attention in my callow youth. I even understood it and memorized it. (My parents and teachers worried.)

Last night I held a lovely hand
A hand so fair and sweet.
I thought my heart would surely burst
The way that it did beat.
No other hand unto my heart could greater pleasure bring
Than the hand I held last night
Four aces and a king.

But as the years, and a few seminary classes, went by I realized that the poetry of hymns began to mean so much to me. I'm still not a poetry aficionado, but show me a great hymn or the Book of Psalms and I'm right with you.

Once our church choir sang a song that really touched my heart. Sure the music was beautiful and majestically sung. But it was the words penned by Robert Browning that touched my heart. I thought that if a poem could make even *me* appreciate more the love of God, you might enjoy it too.

ENCOURAGE

Read it slowly. The first three stanzas are Browning talking to himself--or to us. In the last verse he turns his gaze to God and speaks words that are words we might also say to God.

God Thou Art Love
Robert Browning

If I forget, yet God remembers.
If these hands of mine cease from their clinging,
Yet the hands divine hold me so firmly, I cannot fall.
And if sometimes I am too tired to call for Him to help me
Then He reads the prayer unspoken in my heart
and lifts my care.
I dare not fear since certainly I know
That I am in God's keeping
Shielded so, from all that else would harm.
And in the hour of stern temptation.
My soul a calm sure hiding place has found:
The everlasting arms my life surround, My life surround!
God thou art love.
I build my faith on that.
I know thee who has kept my path.
And made light for me in the darkness
Tempering sorrow so that it reached me like a solemn joy.
It were too strange that I should doubt thy love.

That is *your* heavenly Father and he loves you. Be encouraged,

Note: To hear a wonderful choir sing this, just Google "God Thou Art Love".

Something to think about before you close this book today:

Read Browning's poem again and write here two or three of God's actions that he mentions which mean the most to you today. Then thank God that that is who he is.

ENCOURAGE

Who Are You?

A few months ago my wife, Joy, and two friends took Entrust's "Developing a Discerning Heart" course. Last week she was going over the textbook again and read for me something that that had encouraged her. It was truths taken from Neil Anderson's <u>Victory Over the Darkness</u> (Ventura, CA; Regal Books, 1990, pp.45-47, 57-59). I was encouraged as I listened to Joy read to me thoughts on "Who I Am" and thought you might also be encouraged if you read and meditated on these biblical truths. It is probably too much to try to take this all in with a onetime quick reading. I'd recommend taking about five or ten of these truths a day, read the scriptures listed with them, and then answer this question for each of them: *So what that this is what I am?* Then talk to God about what came to your mind. This will take several days, but I think you will be glad you took the effort and time to do it.

WHO I AM

I am the salt of the earth (Matt. 5:13).

I am the light of the world (Matt. 5:14).

I am a child of God (Jn. 1:12).

I am Christ's friend (Jn. 15:15).

I am a slave of righteousness (Rom. 8:16).

I am a joint heir with Christ, sharing His inheritance with Him (Rom. 8:17).

I am a temple—a dwelling place—of God. His Spirit and His life dwell in me. (1 Cor. 3:16; 6:19)

I am a member of Christ's body (I Cor. 12:27; Eph. 5:30).

ENCOURAGE

I am a new creation (2 Cor. 5:17).

I am reconciled to God and am a minister of reconciliation (2 Cor. 5:18-19).

I am a saint (Eph.1:1; 1 Cor. 1:2; Phil. 1:1; Col. 1:2).

I am God's workmanship—His handiwork—born anew in Christ to do His work (Eph. 2:10).

I am a fellow citizen with the rest of God's family (Eph. 2:19).

I am a prisoner of Christ (Eph. 3:1; 4:1).

I am righteous and holy (Eph. 4:24).

I am a citizen of heaven, seated in heaven right now (Phi. 3:20; Eph. 2:6).

I am hidden with Christ in God (Col.3:3).

I am chosen of God, holy and dearly loved (Col.3:12; 1 Thes. 1:4).

I am a partaker of Christ; I share in His life (Heb. 3:14).

I am one of God's living stones, being built up in Christ as a spiritual house (1 Peter 2:5).

I am a member of a chosen race, a royal priesthood, a holy nation, a people for God's own possession (1 Pet. 2:9-10).

I am an alien and stranger in this world in which I temporarily live (1 Pet. 2:11).

I am an enemy of the devil (1 Pet. 5:8).

I am born of God, and the evil one—the devil—cannot touch me (1 Jn. 5:18).

I have been justified—completely forgiven and made righteous (Rom. 5:18).

ENCOURAGE

I died with Christ and died to the power of sin's rule over my life (Rom. 6:1-6).

I am free forever from condemnation (Rom. 8:1).

I have received the Spirit of Christ into my life that I might know the things freely given to me by God ((1 Cor. 2:12).

I have been given the mind of Christ (1 Cor. 2:16).

I have been bought with a price; I am not my own; I belong to God (1 Cor. 6:19-20).

Since I have died, I no longer live for myself, but for Christ (2 Cor. 5:14-15).

I have been crucified with Christ and it is no longer I who live, but Christ lives in me. The life I am now living is Christ's life (Gal. 2:20).

I have been blessed with every spiritual blessing (Eph.1:3).

I was chosen in Christ before the foundation of the world to be holy and am without blame before Him (Eph. 1:4).

I was predestined—determined by God—to be adopted as God's son (Eph.1:5).

I have been raised up and seated with Christ in heaven (Eph. 2:6).

I have direct access to God through the Spirit (Eph.2:18).

I may approach God with boldness, freedom and confidence (Eph.3:12).

I have been rescued from the domain of Satan's rule and transferred to the kingdom of Christ (Col. 1:13).

I have been redeemed and forgiven of all my sins. The debt against me has been canceled. (Col. 1:14).

Christ Himself is in me (Col. 1:27).

ENCOURAGE

I have been made complete in Christ (Col. 2:10).

I have been buried, raised and made alive with Christ (Col. 2:12-13).

I have died with Christ and I have been raised up with Christ. My life is now hidden with Christ in God. Christ is now my life (Col. 3:1-4).

I have been given a spirit of power, love and self-discipline (2 Tim. 1:7).

I have been saved and set apart according to God's doing (2 Tim. 1:9; Titus 3:5).

I have the right to come boldly before the throne of God to find mercy and grace in time of need (Heb. 4:16).

I have been given exceedingly great and precious promises by God by which I am a partaker of God's divine nature (2 Pet. 1:4).

It that the way you think about yourself? That is who you are and that is the way God thinks about you. Amazing! Wonderful!

ENCOURAGE

Your Ministry May Produce Giants of Faith

In 1900 there was no more famous missionary than John Paton. Today few Christians have even heard of his name. Sometimes an old and forgotten story, like that of John Paton, reasserts itself as a fresh, new insight for *our* day and needs.

John Paton was a missionary to the New Hebrides, circa 1860. In one chapter of his biography, he movingly wrote of two new Christians who renounced their former cannibalism and idol worship: Namuri and Abraham.

Abraham had been a Christian a few years, but was already a teacher of the Bible with John Paton on the island of Tanna. One time Paton had such severe attacks of malaria, he concluded he was dying. He told how Abraham carried him to a safe place and slowly nursed him back to health. That was just one example of what kind of person Abraham was. Paton wrote:

"That noble soul, Abraham, stood by me as an angel of God in sickness and in danger; he went at my side wherever I had to go; he helped me willingly to the last inch of strength in all that I had to do; and it was perfectly manifest that he was doing all this not from mere human love, but for the sake of Jesus. That man had been a cannibal in his heathen days, but by the grace of God there he stood verily a new creature in Christ Jesus. In trial or danger, I was often refreshed by that old teacher's prayers, as I used to be by the prayers of my saintly father. No person could have been a more valuable helper to me in my perilous circumstances; and no person could have shown more fearless and chivalrous devotion."

The reason I quoted this is that Paton had been hearing of some comments of people back in Scotland who hinted that his mission was a waste. He wrote, "All the skepticism of Europe should hide its head in foolish shame; and all its doubts would dissolve under one glance of the new light that Jesus pours from that converted cannibal's eyes."

Namuri, another former cannibal and now Christian teacher, went to a village near where Paton was and "led amongst the heathen a pure and humble Christian life. Without books or a school he instructed them in divine things." A native *sacred man* saw Namuri's increasing influence and attacked him. Namuri barely escaped with his life and fled to Paton's house. It took a month before he could walk again and soon desired to return to his post. Paton pled with him to remain at the mission house. He replied,

"When I see them thirsting for my blood, I just see myself when the missionary first came to my island. I desired to murder him, as they now desire to kill me. Had he stayed away for such danger, I would have remained Heathen; but he came and continued coming to teach us, till, by the grace of God, I was changed to what I am. Now the same God, who changed me to this, can change these poor Tannese to love and serve Him. I cannot stay away from them."

ENCOURAGE

Namuri returned to his village work and for several weeks things appeared most encouraging. More people showed growing interest. But one morning, while Namuri was kneeling in prayer, that same *priest* sprang upon him with his club and left him for dead. Namuri recovered enough to crawl to the mission house. As he was dying there, he constantly prayed for his attackers, *"O Lord Jesus, forgive them, for they know not what they are doing. Oh, take not away all Thy servants from Tanna! Take not away Thy Worship from this dark island! O God, bring all the Tannese to love and follow Jesus."*

Paton wrote, "Humble though he may appear in the world's esteem, I knew that a great man had fallen there in the service of Christ, and that he would take rank in the glorious Army of the Martyrs." The missionary stood humbly before the grave of the former cannibal, honored that he had been used by God to have a part in the spiritual growth of such a person.

For our generation, you are the John Patons. And some of those who follow Christ, in part because of your time with them, are like Abraham and Namuri, who will also do great things for the kingdom. Their life, and perhaps their death, will glorify God in wonderful ways. And just think, God called *you* and your family to have a part in all that through whatever ministry God has given you.

Not every Hebrides convert became an Abraham or Namuri. Some were pretty nominal and some went back to their pagan ways. But others continued with the Lord and reached out to others so that thirty years later every island in the New Hebrides had a strong church; today over 90% of the population call themselves Christians.

John Paton did not know how many of those he worked with would become strong, multiplying followers of Christ. At times his work seemed barren. At times there was strong opposition from heathen priests, the English and French traders, and at times, from misguided people back home. There was sickness and death, problems with the government, lack of funds and emotional depression, but Paton knew that God had called him to work among those people, and he persevered. And now and then an Abraham or a Namuri came forth.

May our loving Lord, our conquering King, support you as you seek to be faithful in however He has called you to serve him.

ENCOURAGE

Be encouraged

An assignment for today:

Read the story of Namuri to someone and discuss it together.

Worry Without Ceasing Vs. Praying Without Ceasing

One day I was talking with my wife over a cup of coffee. She is the sensitive, creative, loving one in the family. She mentioned that she had been thinking about some of the difficulties our son and daughter-in-law must be having as new missionaries in South America. Then her concerns included our son-in law and his new, unusual, undiagnosed physical symptoms. And don't forget about our friend's marriage problems, I was reminded.

I realized that that kind of caring thinking was going on in Joy's mind *all the time*. Actually some of that, and other things as well, were always going on in my mind too. I'm sure you've noticed that our minds are *always* active: we analyze, reflect, worry, ponder and day-dream. There's not a moment when we're not thinking. Some of it continues to trouble our dreams.

Henri Nouwen, noted that our thinking is *unceasing*. It would be nice, so we imagine, if we could just turn off the static, the cacophony, for a while and just stop thinking...*for a while*. That solitude would rescue us from our always bringing to mind worries, guilt feelings and fears. Our ability to think obviously is a great gift from God, but too often we can turn our worrisome thoughts into great pain. Thus, in much of our lives we can be victims of our unceasing thoughts.

But it doesn't have to be that way. Nouwen wrote that we could convert our unceasing thinking into unceasing prayer by making our inner *monologue* into a continuing *dialogue* with God--who is the source of all love. He leads us beside the still waters.

The Apostle Paul encourages us to pray *without ceasing*. So as we turn our monologue-thinking into a dialogue with God we can pray *without ceasing*. That's what Brother Laurence meant by *the practice of the presence of God*.

When we find ourselves *worrying* about something, we can immediately turn that worry into a *conversation* with God. Nouwen continued: "Let's break out of our isolation and realize that Someone who dwells in the center of our being wants to listen with love to all that occupies and preoccupies our minds."

Thus, we can discover a bit more what it means to live an abundant life as we move from unceasing worry to unceasing prayer.

Be encouraged. God is waiting for that conversation with you.

Something to think about before you close this book today What is buzzing around in your thoughts today that you should share with your heavenly Father.

ENCOURAGE

God Was Here

One of my desires has been that I would be more aware of God's presence throughout the day. I can remember sharing with some men in a discipleship group I attended that sometimes a day would go by and I hadn't thought of God for most of it after my morning devotions.

I started getting Skye Jathani's email daily devotional recently. Skye was the director of Mission Advancement for "Christianity Today." Recently he mentioned something Ignatius Loyola taught his followers. It was a very simple practice to aid Christians in their awareness of God's presence. Before going to sleep each night, he instructed his followers to recall the events of their day from beginning to end—their activities, conversations, feelings and struggles. In doing this they were to ask, "Lord, show me how you were with me today."

Skye wrote, "Looking back, one might discover his presence in a moment of kindness, in a scene of beauty, in the joy of a stranger's smile, or amid the pain of a loss."

I am not good at reflecting. I run through a day and it becomes a flurry of action and thoughts. As Skye pointed out, "Like a speeding car, we race ahead and rarely notice the scenes we are passing though." I have tried several times to do what Ignatius Loyola recommended. I haven't done it well, but trying to recall the day's journey helped me notice God's presence in some of the events of the day.

James Martin said, "It's easier to see God in retrospect rather than in the moment." And I want to see God more clearly, see how he is involved in my life and therefore to love and appreciate him more and give him the praise he deserves.

In Psalm 73:23, 26, David wrote, "Yet I am always with you; you hold me by my right hand. You guide me with your counsel...My flesh and my heart may fail, but God is the strength of my heart and my portion forever." This view of God's presence came about after David took time one day to reflect on the apparent easy life some wicked people had and then what their end was. He compared that with how God had been faithful to him and that reflection cause him to love and praise God even more.

You probably remember that story in 2 Kings 6:15-17 when Elisha's servant saw the army of the king of Aram surrounding them. He panicked but Elisha asked the Lord to open the servant's eyes. When he did the servant "looked and saw the hills full of horses and chariots of fire all around them." Sometimes when we ask God to help us see where he has been with us, we recognize that we have been protected in many wonderful ways.

In Genesis 28, Jacob slept on the ground in a certain place and he had a vision of God. "When Jacob awoke from his sleep, he thought, 'Surely the Lord is in this place, and I was not aware of it.'" If we take the time to reflect on our day, we too may discover that the Lord has been with us and we did not know it.

Be encouraged. He has always been with you and will always be with you.

Something you can do to help you recollect God's presence in your life: Try for a few days to follow Ignatius Loyola's teaching to his followers. I kept forgetting to do that so I put a note on my dresser that said, "Don't forget to recall events of the day and ask the Lord to show you how he was with you today. I still forget, but the note does sometimes help.

Speaking as a Resident Alien

I want to give a few words of challenge to you resident aliens who are reading this. Some of you may remember singing: *This world is not my home. I'm just a passin' through.* The first line of that song is accurate, but the second isn't. Christians are **not** *just a passin' through.*

In 2 Corinthians 5:8 Paul speaks of preferring to be "at home with the Lord." Don't we all? But a few verses later (vs. 20) he points out why he is willing to stay away from his home. "We are therefore Christ's ambassadors..." He is an ambassador to this world representing God's kingdom. He is not living in this world and *just a passin' through* until he is called home.. He has been given an important position to fulfill for his King.

Webster's New Collegiate Dictionary says that an ambassador is: a diplomatic agent of the highest rank accredited to a foreign government as the resident representative of his own government or sovereign or appointed for a special and often temporary diplomatic assignment.

That last phrase fits us. We have been appointed by our sovereign for a special, temporary assignment. The Great Commission sums up well the central part of our assignment: "...make disciples of all nations..." Our time on earth should be focused on carrying out the assignment we have been given by our Sovereign.

When Paul called himself and us Christ's ambassadors, he spoke of God committing to us "the message of reconciliation." We have been given "the ministry of reconciliation" (2 Cor. 5:18). We express this "ministry" as we do whatever work God has called us to do wherever he has called us to do it.

When someone from a foreign country comes to the United States to live and work here for a while, they apply for a "green card." Once they get this "Permanent Resident Card." They can live, work and move around the country freely. In a sense we can think of ourselves as permanent residents of the United States. If we have a green card, we can live and work wherever and represent our true Sovereign in all we do.

We are not *just a passin' through* this life. Our King has appointed us to represent him to those with whom he brings us into contact. We are a high ranking diplomatic representative of the King of Kings. He has important work for us to do.

We need to keep in close communication with our King and discover the joy of serving as his ambassadors in this place which is not our actual home. Be encouraged. You are Christ's ambassador who has been given a very important assignment.

Something to think about before you close this book today:

What specific assignment has your King given you that you are now working on?

The Balanced Christian Life

Early in my new life as a follower of Christ at the University of Illinois, I was given some Navigator discipleship materials. One part of the studies I did concerned "The Wheel." This was a diagram that pictured the balanced Christian life.

This diagram was developed by Navigators' founder and first president Dawson Trotman to help others remember basic principles of the Christian life. In the 1930s he used a three-legged stool—the legs representing prayer, the Word, and witnessing. But he became dissatisfied with the illustration; it left the Christian sitting down! So he developed the concept into a wheel. The truths illustrated in "The Wheel" were quite instrumental in my early growth as a Christian.

The Hub: Christ the Center

The key to living a victorious, Spirit-filled Christian life is to keep Jesus Christ as the center and Lord of all we do. Now that I have been of follower of Christ for over half a century, I realize even more vividly that this is the key to a balanced Christian life. Just as the driving force in a wheel comes from the hub, so the power to live the Christian life comes from Jesus. The more I relate everything I do to loving Jesus, the stronger a disciple I become.

There are two **vertical spokes.** These are how you relate to God. The first one is the **Word.** The Bible is our spiritual food and our sword for spiritual battle. Study of and meditation on scripture is foundational for effective Christian living. I had been a Christian for about 13 years when someone challenged me to not let a day go by when I did not spend time reading God's Word. Nothing has been more valuable to my life than doing that.

The second vertical spoke is **Prayer**. Prayer is opening every part of your life to God who desires to have a close relationship with you and who cares about your concerns. It unleashes God's power in our lives and the lives of those we pray for.

There are two **horizontal spokes**. These are how you relate to others. The first is **Witnessing**. (I would rather label this **witnessing and service**.) Jesus' last words to his disciples concern helping others come to receive this new life in Christ and helping others in need.

Fellowship is the second horizontal spoke. (I would rather label this **fellowship and disciple making**). The Christian life is not just a solitary (God and me) experience. We are called to help love, pray for, encourage and build up fellow believers.

The Rim: Obedience to Christ

The rim of a wheel is where "the rubber meets the road." The rim represents the Christian responding to Christ's lordship and the Holy Spirit's promptings through wholehearted, day-to-day obedience to Him. People can do religious things like Bible reading and prayer and not obey what promptings they receive. Obedience to God's leading is a decision we continually have to make.

Now why have I put this all down in writing? How can this be encouraging to you? This morning as I talked with a friend about "The Wheel," I realized that I have let one or more of the spokes at times get short. When that happens the tire is flat on one side and my life goes flop, flop, flop. But as we keep Christ at the center of our life and obey his Word and the Holy Spirit's promptings and keep all four spokes strong, our Christian life is empowered and runs much smoother (though there will be rough roads) and we slowly come closer to our goal of conformity to the image of Christ. I hope that is encouraging.

Some questions to think about before you close this book today:

1. *Is your connection to the hub strong?*
2. *Which of your spokes needs strengthening so the wheel doesn't get lopsided?*

The Lord Gives Strength to His People

Whenever a new year begins, I get excited about what God has ahead. But I know living for Christ in today's world will not be easy. I am going to need help from someone stronger than I am. God is all-powerful. Most of us don't have any problem with thinking about him as all-powerful, but we often wonder... so what's that mean for me?

Psalm 29:1-11 helps us there. It not only points out the powerfulness of God but also that he wants to share his power with us. He promises to give us power to deal with whatever comes into our life. *"The Lord gives strength to his people; the Lord blesses his people with peace."* He wants to equip and empower his people, you and me, so that we can find peace when we're panicking and find endurance when we're empty and find courage when we're cowardly, He can help us with the will power to avoid doing things we shouldn't do and to do the things we know we should do. Now the big question is: How do we access his power when tragedy strikes, when we're lured by temptation, or when we want to grow in Christ-likeness? I want to mention several things that might help.

I Chronicles 16:11-12 says, *"Look to the Lord and his strength. Seek his face always. Remember the wonders he has done. Remember his miracles."* I have found it helpful to take time to think back and **remember situations when God has come through in wonderful ways.** For the last few years my wife, Joy, has been writing down stories she remembers of God's working in our lives. We have found that just remembering those things has been very encouraging and strengthening.

Another thing that has been a great help to me through the years is reading Christian biographies like those of Jim Elliott, Brother Andrew,

ENCOURAGE

Mother Teresa, David Livingstone, Corrie ten Boom, John Wesley, and John Calvin. Recently I have read several books by former Muslims who have come to Christ through many difficulties. Through these stories I was reminded that God is not some distant, detached and disinterested deity. He was a very real presence in those people's lives and he can be that in mine and in yours. Get a good Christian biography this month and start reading. Also reading and thinking about what God did for his people in the Bible does the same thing.

The next step is to admit your own weakness. So often when a difficulty or a temptation comes, our reaction is to try to get through it on our own. The reality is that we cannot be filled with the power of God until we first empty ourselves of the pretense that we can make it through on our own. God can only fill empty vessels. When we admit our helplessness and weakness, then we can really open our hearts to God.

Thirdly, align yourself with God's will. Some people think God's power is like an electrical outlet that we plug into when we want to and receive power for whatever purpose we want. But God's power doesn't work that way. Jesus said in John 15:5, *"I'm the vine, you are the branches. Whoever remains in me and I in him will bear much fruit."* There is a big difference between an electric cord and a wall outlet and a branch and a vine. Moment by moment we need to be connected with God as a branch is to the vine. Align yourself with God's will and walk down the road God wants you to walk on. Then as you keep putting one foot in front of the other, God will give you strength to take the next step.

Fourthly, ask God for the power you need. The Bible tells us, *"You have not because you ask not."* We cannot move through life just assuming God is going to take care of us and give us the strength we need to face whatever comes. Stay in close touch with God. If you humbly ask for help and guidance in a situation, He will give it.

The fifth step may be the most important: **act right now in obedience to God.** There's a pattern in scripture that even if we don't feel empowered, we're still to take action by obediently proceeding on the road God wants us to walk. As we do he promises to give us strength as strength is needed. When we do that, we are demonstrating faith. Faith is not just believing some facts. Faith is belief plus behavior, belief plus actions. Faith is always a verb in the Bible, not a noun. Someone said that if you

62

ENCOURAGE

were taking a picture of faith it would come out blurred because it would be moving as you took the picture.

Some of you have read the book God's Smuggler, by Brother Andrew. During the Cold War days, he believed God had called him to get Bibles to people behind the Iron Curtain who desperately wanted them but could not get them. He said, "Here's how it happened. I would pray and would sense God leading me to a particular country, a closed society. My advisors would pray too and we would come to an agreement, 'Yes, this is the country God wants us to bring Bibles into.' When we came to that realization, I often didn't feel great boldness, or tremendous courage, I was scared stiff. I didn't feel like God had suddenly infused me with a great ability or great power of courage. What I would do is walk in obedience down the road toward the border of that country with the Bibles. Time after time in the most amazing way the door to that country would swing open and God would find a way for me to get those Bibles into that country. God gave the strength to do it, the power to do it, the ability to do it as I needed it along the way of obedience."

He continued, "It's sort of like a supermarket door. If you're sitting in the parking lot at a supermarket and look at the door, you could sit there all day and wish and hope but the door is not going to open as a result of you mentally trying to make it open. But if you begin to walk toward that door in faith, you know you're not going to bump into that door because as you approach the door there's a sensor that will know you're approaching and the door is going to open. It opens because you're walking in faith toward the door. That's basically the principle I've lived by all these years. God is waiting for us to walk forward in obedience so he can open the door for us to serve him."

Is there an area in your life where you've gone through the first four steps of how to get God's power, but you're still afraid? I would say, take action. When we demonstrate faith by taking specific steps of obedience, even when we don't feel empowered by God, he will supernaturally empower us.

Here are five steps to take when you need God's power. He knows where you need his strength. He knows where you are in your life. The amazing thing about God is that he doesn't see us as just a bunch of humans. He sees individual lives, people he cares for and loves. And God just doesn't see what you've been. He sees what you can be. He sees you for who you will become, if day by day you walk these five steps, receive his strength and power and follow that path he has for your life.

Just consider the possibilities of life like that. God already has.

Something to think about before you close this book today:

Which of these five steps is the most difficult for you? I there any place in your life today where you need to put the fifth step into practice?

Most difficult: _____

Area where fifth step is needed: _____

When Troubles Hit

For years friends of mine have been involved in ministry to Haiti, drilling wells to provide clean water, building schools and churches, sending money to provide school costs for young Haitians and more. Their stories of the poverty there would touch anyone's heart. But then in mid-January 2010, a 7.0 earthquake hit near the capital city and tens of thousands died and millions found themselves living in a destroyed city. Their previous life of poverty seemed to be good compared with their situation now. One tragedy has been piled upon another.

Tragedy hit thousands in Haiti. Sometimes the sorrows of life pile upon one person out of many. We see that pictured for us in the book of Ruth, one tragedy piled upon another. Trouble number one was a famine in Israel, so bad that Elimelech and his family went to a neighboring country and became refugees. Trouble number two was having to live as a refugee. Then trouble or rather tragedy number three hit. Elimelech died and his wife, Naomi, was left raising two sons. Being a single, refugee mother was not easy. The two boys grew up and married local girls. Ah, a bit of good news. But then tragedies numbers four and five hit. Both boys died and widow Naomi was left with two young widow daughters-in-law. One tragedy piled upon another upon another upon another.

I doubt that any of us will ever have to face famine and the loss of spouse and children or face what our brothers and sisters in Christ in Haiti have been hit with. But still this is a fallen world and we are fallen people living among other fallen people. That combination leads each of us to have to face all kinds of troubles, tragedies and disappointments. There are illnesses, accidents, economic troubles, disappointments and family strife. Often one trouble is piled upon another.

ENCOURAGE

How did Naomi face her tragedies? She heard that the famine was over in Israel and she decided to go back home. One daughter-in-law stayed in Moab, but the other, Ruth, chose to go with her mother-in-law. When Naomi, which means pleasant, arrived in her hometown, Bethlehem, she told her neighbors not to call her Naomi, but Mara, which means bitter, "for the Almighty has made life very bitter for me. I went away full but the Lord has brought me home empty."

At times when trouble hits me and life caves in, I respond like Naomi. Negativity, depression, poor me, anger and more grow up in my heart and spirit. I begin concentrating on myself. "Call me Mara. I once was full, but now I am empty.

But was Naomi empty? No. Many tragedies had hit her, but remember Ruth was there. And also God had Boaz, a relative, who would help. God had not left Naomi alone. Her Heavenly Father would never do that. She was not empty. And it wasn't long before she held Ruth's little baby, Obed, King David's great-grandfather, in her arms and the women of Bethlehem said to her, "Praise the Lord...your daughter-in-law who loves you so much...has been better to you than seven sons!"

I cannot imagine what those in Haiti have had to face. We should pray for people in such situations and give what we can to help them. But God's Word is still true. He is our comforter and fortress, our source of strength and hope. He promises to give us the help we need to not give up. Experiences of deep sorrow, pain and trouble can spread a shadow over the face of our lives. The darkness of grief and pain can leave us feeling emotionally and spiritually paralyzed. I am sure many in Haiti have felt like that. We need to keep in our prayers those facing such troubles that they might know God's comfort and strength so that they do not ask people to call them Mara and think of themselves as empty and without hope.

When earthquakes hit that devastate thousands or troubles of some kind hit us, the same truth can be our comfort. Our loving heavenly Father will never leave us alone. Jesus said, "I am with you always." When these terrible times come, his Spirit will be with us in a special way. And if we look around, we will also see there are other good gifts of God right there. Like David, we can always say, "You have allowed me to suffer much hardship, but you will restore me to life again and lift me up from the depths of the earth. You will...comfort me once again...you are faithful to your promises, O my God" (Ps. 71:20-21).

Something to think about before you close this book today.

This is a fallen world. We all face difficulties, disappointment and troubles. What could you say to a friend who right now is in the midst of a very difficult situation? How can you share these truths without sounding trite?

A Blessing of Salvation: Hope

Charles Spurgeon said of Puritan Thomas Brooks that he "scatters stars with both his hands." In 1654, Brooks published *Heaven on Earth, a Treatise on Christian Assurance*. In it he noted that *hope* is one of the blessings that accompany salvation. He then described seven properties of that hope. Below are four of them. May Brooks' thoughts encourage and cheer you today.

Hope raises the heart to live above, where its treasure is.

Since we are now living on this earth, it is sometimes difficult to turn our attentions to things more real. The hope that accompanies our salvation helps us do that. Just think, one day we will be with Christ. Hope takes the pleasures of heaven beforehand and helps us live in joyful expectation. Brooks calls it *the sweet anticipation of heaven*, and describes it as this... *divine hope that enables us to turn our thoughts from the things of earth to heaven where we receive new life to make us truly alive, and gives wisdom to guide us, power to strengthen us, righteousness to justify us, mercy to forgive us and assurance to rejoice us.* It helps us, in a sense, to live above-- and not just on--this fallen earth.

Hope that accompanies salvation strengthens us in all afflictions and temptations.

The men and women mentioned in Hebrews 11 had a hope of possessing at last *"a house not made with hands, but eternal in the heavens."* Those hopes made them willing and cheerful to live in deserts and mountains and in dens and caves. Our hope also enables us to withstand our strong temptations and troubles. We can truly say, "My hopes are better than my possessions." Brooks wrote, *"We have much in promise but little in purse."* Roman's 5:2-5 tells us that we can rejoice in our sufferings because they produce *perseverance* which leads to *character* and produces *hope*.

And hope does not disappoint us. It is not just unfounded optimism but is based on the love and power of God.

Hope gives us great quietness in the midst of all storms.

Hebrews 6:19 says, *"We have this hope as an anchor for the soul, firm and secure."* Hope is the anchor that enables us to be quiet and secure in all storms and keeps us from being dashed upon the rocks.

Once, years ago when I was in the navy, I was on watch one night and our ship was at anchor. A strong wind rose and the anchor began to drag. Fortunately, I was able to accomplish maneuvers that kept us out of major trouble. But I didn't feel secure that whole night till the wind died down in the morning. I didn't feel very secure for that anchor was only fastened down ten meters and in sand. Our hope, happily, is anchored in heaven, not on earth. We will not be moved, even when a storm comes.

Hope causes the soul to wait patiently for delayed mercy.

Romans 4:18-21 tells us that *"Abraham in hope believed...just as it had been said to him."* Hope often enables us wait for a mercy. Brooks said well, *"The longer I wait for a mercy, the greater, better and sweeter, at last, the mercy will prove, says hope. It is not mercy, if it be not worth waiting for, says hope; and if it be a mercy, thou canst not wait too long for it, says hope."* Hope does not tell God when he must show mercy but leaves to the One who is faithful and true both the time and manner he will act. Christ knows his own time and though he delays, hope knows he will certainly come and will not wait a moment beyond his perfect time.

May we know in our hearts what Paul prayed for his friends:

> *"...that your hearts will be flooded with light so that you can understand the wonderful future he has promised to those he has called. I want you to realize what a rich and glorious inheritance he has given to his people."*
>
> *"I pray that you will begin to understand the incredible greatness of his power for us who believe him. This is the same mighty power that raised Christ from the dead and seated him in the place of honor....!"* (Ephesians 1:18-20 NLT).

Something to think about before you close this book today:

How would you explain what Christian hope is to a friend who thinks of hope as just a positive attitude?

ENCOURAGE

All Your Earthly Possessions in a Nine-Year-Old Ford

My son and his wife, career missionaries, lived in Mexico for ten years when they were in their thirties and forties. They have no children and that makes a difference in many ways, but their lifestyle still challenges me. Those ten years they lived in a cold, unheated 450 square foot (20'x 22') house in a city 9000 feet high. One time my wife asked our daughter-in-law, who grew up in a doctor's home, "Have you outgrown your little house?" She answered, "Actually, I've grown into it."

Once as we were strolling through a "craft fair" in their city in Mexico, I pointed out a lovely little handmade item. My daughter-in-law, who also thought it was attractive and creative, said, "What a nice little dustable." They had no room in their little home for another "dustable," so she wasn't even tempted to buy it.

When they finished their work in Mexico, we helped them move their possessions. We took with us four forty-pound suitcases. Another couple did the same thing. All the rest of their earthly possessions, and I emphasize "earthly", they packed in their nine-year-old Ford Explorer.

I look at the thirty or forty year olds in the community where we live, I see many of them living in a mortgaged house just a little more expensive than they can afford, driving two cars and paying two monthly payments on them and having several credit cards close to maxed out. With all that debt, they certainly can't tithe and they are always facing financial pressures.

Most Americans, probably most Christian Americans, would look and our son and daughter-in-law and feel sorry for them. "Poor missionaries, they have nothing." But when we were with them, I saw a different picture. I saw some of the results of their ministry in Mexico. I saw people so grateful for what they had done with and for them. There were going away parties with tears shed because they were leaving.

I really don't know anyone more satisfied with their life than these two, even though they "have almost nothing." In reality, friends of theirs in

71

ENCOURAGE

the states envy them. Their life shows very clearly that things, possessions, bank accounts and the like are not the source of happiness or fulfillment.

Let me encourage you as one who has seen so clearly an example of what really makes life meaningful. It is not possessions, position, titles or wealth. It is a relationship with God and doing what he has called us to do, where he has called us to do it.

My wife did a study in Ecclesiastes and in that book Solomon shows so clearly that God is the one who directs our lives as he wills, for his glory. Some are called to live in a 450 square foot house and others are called to have and oversee a multi-million-dollar foundation. If the Bible is true, and I believe it is, both those people can live a joyous, fulfilled, meaningful life and enjoy God's presence and blessings right where they are.

Let me share with you a prayer by Jeremy Taylor (1613-1667).

Let no riches make me ever forget myself, no poverty make me to forget you; let no hope or fear, no pleasure or pain, no accident without, no weakness within, hinder or decompose my duty, or turn me from the ways of your commandments. O let your Spirit dwell with me forever, and make my soul just and charitable, full of honesty, full of religion, resolute and constant in holy purpose, but inflexible to evil. Make me humble and obedient, peaceable and pious; let me never envy any man's good, nor deserve to be despised myself and if I be, teach me to bear it with meekness and charity

.

Something to think about before you close this book today:

If someone looked at my house, car(s), checkbook, and credit card statements, what might they come to conclude about what I believe is the source of happiness or fulfillment?

ENCOURAGE

Are You Excited About Heaven?

I've often wondered what heaven is going to be like. The Bible doesn't, at first glance, seem to say much about it. That was okay because I knew that what God has in store for believers will be far better than I can imagine. It'll be wonderful! But still, I've often thought: what is it going to be like?

Then I read Randy Alcorn's excellent book, <u>Heaven</u>. In it he shows how much there is in the Bible about what Heaven will be like. I've read through the Bible many times, but missed much that it teaches about where we'll spend eternity and what it will be like. What Alcorn showed was in the scriptures was absolutely exciting.

I am really excited now about dying. (I think I'd better put that differently.) I'm certain God still has things for me to do. But now I'm a lot more excited than I was about how I am going to be able to serve God on His new earth and new Heaven, and how fantastic eternity is going to be.

It is interesting that though a high percentage of Americans believe in the resurrection of the dead, two thirds believe they will not have bodies after the resurrection. How wrong they are. A non-physical resurrection is like a sunless sunrise. The Westminster Confession teaches us to affirm: *All the dead shall be raised up, with the self-same bodies, and none other."*

Paul in his letter to the Philippians (3:20-21) writes, *"The Lord Jesus Christ...will transform our lowly bodies so that they will be like his glorious body."*

And will heaven be boring? That famous literary character, Huck Finn, spoke of Miss Watson, a Christian spinster, who told him about the good place. *"She said all a body would have to do there was to go around all day long with a harp and sing, forever and ever. So I didn't think much of it. I asked her if she reckoned Tom Sawyer would go there and she said, not by a considerable sight. I was glad about that because I wanted him and me to be together."*

ENCOURAGE

Huck would have had a different response, I speculate, if Miss Watson told him what the Bible says about having a perfected, resurrected body and our being with people we love on a renewed and perfect earth with gardens and rivers and mountains and untold adventures. Hebrews 11 describes our eternal future residence as a city and a country. "City" suggests buildings and art, culture and music, goods and services and athletics. "Countries" have diverse people and rivers, mountains, trees and flowers.

John Piper wrote, *"God promises that the glory of his people will demand a glorious creation to live in. so the fallen creation will obtain the very freedom from futility and evil and pain that the church is given...he makes us new physically and spiritually and then makes the whole creation new so that our environment fits our perfected spirits and bodies."*

The new earth will be better than Eden because heaven and earth will be united as never before, as Anthony Hoekema wrote," *God will make the new earth his dwelling place...Heaven and earth will then no longer be separated as they are now. But they will be one."*

Revelation 21:3 identifies that, *"God himself will be with us."* God, not a designate, will be with us. Steve Lawson writes: *"God's glory will fill and permeate the entire new Heaven, not just one centralized place. Wherever we go, we will enjoy the complete manifestation of God's presence, unhindered fellowship with God."*

Will we always be engaged in worship in heaven? Randy Alcorn answers: *"Yes and no. If we have a narrow view of worship, the answer is no. If we have a broad view of worship, the answer is yes. Will we always be at Christ's feet worshipping him? No, the Bible says we will be doing many other things, but all we do will be an act of worship. We'll have full and unbroken fellowship with Christ."*

Have you not worshipped God while walking on the beach at sunset or canoeing on a lake surrounded by the beauty of our world? Those times can be wonderful worship even though they are taking place on a fallen earth and we are fallen, sinful people.

What will worship on the new heaven and earth be like? At times we'll lose ourselves in praise as we look at Jesus' face. At other times, as

ENCOURAGE

Alcorn says, we'll worship him when we *"build a cabinet, paint a picture, cook a meal, talk with a friend, take a walk or throw a ball."*

Be assured, it'll never be boring. We'll never lose our fascination for God even as we get to know him better. J. I. Packer wrote, *"Hearts on earth may say in the course of a joyful experience, 'I don't want this ever to end.' But invariable it does. The hearts of those in heaven will say, 'I want this to go on forever,' And it will. There is no better news that this."*

So when the times are tough and you're tempted to get discouraged, remember....

A question to ask yourself before you close this book today:

In what you read today, what is a new positive, encouraging thought for you?

ENCOURAGE

Christian Hope Is Not Just Hoping

In October 2007 the Dow Jones financial indicator was at a breathtaking 14,165. It continued up and up along with America's craving hopes. Many of us giddily spent and spent, leaving our credit cards gasping.

But March 2008 our mighty market was gasping at 6547. *Wachovia Bank*, which a few years ago was just a frisky upstart in Charlotte, NC, had grown large and went national. Now a smaller bank, *Wells Fargo*, bought *Wachovia* just before its value collapsed.

In 2016 the Dow was as 18,500, but people were still anxious wondering if there would be another big downturn.

Obviously, our national economy has caused a lot of people to live in a state of anxiety. There are friends who have lost their jobs and have never gotten them back. Many people's savings have shrunk. Strong, giant corporations have filed for bankruptcy. These days a lot of casual conversations and party talk centers on the financial situation and anxiety. Again you hear politicians saying, "It's the economy, stupid."

When I was in Iraq in 2015, I never heard an Iraqi believer even mention the worldwide financial troubles. They spoke of sharing their faith with others, of what God was doing in their house churches, of wanting to learn more of the Bible and of the difficulties of being a Christian in a non-Christian culture.

I believe one of the reasons our financial anxiety is so heightened is that we Americans are not used to facing tough times. When things are tough financially, and we see Christianity being marginalized in the U.S.-- and even attacked, we get anxious. But Christ followers have always lived

ENCOURAGE

in cultures that are far from the Kingdom of God's values. Satan is the prince of this world.

How have believers lived victoriously throughout the centuries and not let worry and anxiety rule them? They certainly faced much more than we are now facing and with far less angst. In part, I believe it is that they understood Christian hope in a way that we have long since lost.

In my 1973 *New Collegiate Dictionary, hope* is defined as "desire accompanied by expectation of fulfillment." That's pretty close to what Christian hope is. But the more recent *American Heritage Dictionary* defines hope as "the feeling that…events will turn out for the best."

But the Christian hope that has supported believers over the centuries is not a feeling. The *Dictionary of New Testament Theology* says hope is "always a confident, sure expectation of divine saving actions." Hope comes from the certainty of God's promises. One of the key promises we can hold on to during these times is Romans 8:28, "God works in all things for *the good* of those who love him."

John Piper identified four fruits of Christian hope.

First: Christian hope bears the fruit of true joy. Happiness depends on circumstances, whether your "hap" is good or not. Joy is not dependent on that.

Second: Christian hope produces sacrificial love. Our focus is not just concerned about what happens, but how we can serve others in the middle of it all.

Third: Christian hope yields boldness. We can see the mess the world is in, but we know God will one day bring all that evil to an end. That is why throughout history believers have been able to give their lives, fortunes and popularity to serve and honor Christ throughout the world.

Finally: Christian hope bears the fruit of endurance. Living for Christ will often be very difficult in this fallen world. There will be battles that we lose. *But we can trust in God's promises.* Christ is building his kingdom; He will be victorious.

Sure times may be tough, but as Charles Colson wrote: "When we grab hold of the hope we have in Christ, we will be able to live with the joy, the sacrificial love, the boldness, and the endurance we will need to face the challenges before us."

Don't be discouraged. Christ has risen. He is with us. Like you, I have read the final chapter of The Book. WE WIN!

Something to think about before you close this book today:

Which of his four fruits of Christian hope stands out to you today? Why do you think so?

Contentment...or Not

In 1950 the average American home was 1100 square feet. In 2000 homes typically were a luxurious 2200 square feet...even though families were smaller. Modern bathrooms and walk-in closets are now the size of my childhood bedroom.

"I want a new iphone." Sure, I have a functioning two year old iphone--it works just fine--but that *new* iphone looks great—feels good in my hand. I'm not content anymore with my plain old iphone. Maybe it's because Apple spent millions of advertising dollars when that *must have new* iphone first came out—do ya think?

Then too, I have a great 12-year-old Chevy, with just 100,000 miles on it, runs like a cloud and gets great mileage. But TV is showing the coolest new cars and the car will even stop itself if I forget to. And I'd guess that if I just test drive one, I wouldn't be nearly so content with that *so last year* Chevy. But if I test drive it, they'll give me a FREE *whatchamacallit*; and I don't have one of those!

Each day I am bombarded with advertisements that sow dissatisfaction with what I have and who I am. (YOU too?) No wonder I'm a bit discontented with my old widgets and my old style-less wardrobe.

Obviously, if our contentment is based on what we possess or what our jobs are or what other people think, we can easily get discontented. There must be a better way to live than looking for satisfaction in all those things. The Apostle Paul wrote to his friends in Philippi, "I have learned to be *content* in whatever circumstances I am," whether he was dining with the wealthy or in a dungeon chewing on a stale crust or just barely hanging on to a wrecked ship lost and floating in the Mediterranean. Notice that he told us he was content, not happy, *content*.

Contentment for Paul came from his relationship with Christ. That relationship freed him to take whatever came without discontentment and dissatisfaction. If we know that God loves us and we trust that he has our best interest in mind, we won't need to compare what others have with what we have or worry about what others think of us. Henry Blackaby wrote, "Discontent stems from the sin of ingratitude and a lack of faith that God loves you enough to provide for all that you need."

Friend, we know that God does love us and, to quote Bill Bright, has a wonderful plan for our lives. May we all become more like Paul who wrote, "I've learned to be quite content whatever my circumstances. I'm just as happy with little as with much, with much as with little…Whatever I have, wherever I am, I can make it through anything in the One who makes me who I am" (The Message).

"Operator, will you please tell that very nice salesman that I won't be buying that terrific new car? Yes, the red one. Thank you."

Something to think about before you close this book today:

Read again Blackaby's quote above and think about it for a minute. Ask God for forgiveness if you see any discontent in your thoughts. Thank him that you know he loves you and will provide all that you need.

ENCOURAGE

Count Your Many Blessings

A short term missionary worked for a while in a leper colony. On his final day there, he was leading worship. He asked if anyone had a favorite song. He noticed a woman in the congregation, a leper, who had the most disfigured face he'd ever seen. She had no ears and no nose; her lips were gone. Slowly she raised a fingerless hand and asked, "Can we sing, 'Count Your Many Blessings'?" When I first read that story, it hit me pretty hard. Way too often I am counting other things than the incredible number of blessings I receive each day. Are you ever like that or are you like that lady and ready to sing "Count Your Many Blessings"?

Psalm 23 reminds us: THE LORD IS MY SHEPHERD; I SHALL NOT WANT. That is absolutely true. We have a good shepherd who will meet all our needs. No matter what we are experiencing today, along with that leper we can sing "Count Your Many Blessings" If we get down at times, it is not that we need a change in our circumstances so our attitude is better. If you think that, you are in the prison of want. You have forgotten all that you have in your Shepherd. It is much greater than what you don't have that you think you need.

May I meddle for a moment? What is the one thing separating you from joy? How would you fill in this blank: I will be happy when...? When I am healed? When I am thinner? When I have another child? When my children leave home? When I have more money? When our staff is perfect?

Now, with your answer firmly in mind, answer this. If your ship never comes in, if your dream never comes true, if the situation never changes, could you be happy? If not, then you are sleeping in the cold cell of discontent. You are in the prison of want. You need to remember all that you have in your Shepherd.

You have a loving God who hears you, the power of love behind you, the Holy Spirit within you, and all of heaven ahead of you. If you have the Good Shepherd; you have grace for every sin, direction for every turn, a candle for every corner, and an anchor for every storm. You have everything you need.

And who can take it from you? Can cancer infect your salvation? Can bankruptcy impoverish your prayers? A tornado might take your earthly house, but it won't touch your heavenly home. Isn't that Great!

I recently read challenging words from an Uzbek convert named Bek. "We often face troubles, but still we are praising God. We have a saying, 'If you are arrested, praise God that you have not been beaten. If you are beaten, praise God that you have not been killed. If you are killed, praise God that you are now with Jesus in heaven.'"

Let's get out our hymnbooks and let's sing "Count Your Many Blessings".

Courtesy to a Grumpy Salesclerk

Jesus said we are the light of the world. In <u>Simple Faith</u>, Chuck Swindoll commented on Matthew 5:16. *"Let your light shine before men in such a way that they may see your good works and glorify your Father who is in heaven.'*

(The world) will see "your good works," Jesus said. Like what?
They will hear your courtesy.
They will detect your smile.
They will notice that you stop to thank them.
They will hear you apologize when you are wrong.
They will see you help them when they are struggling.
They will notice that you are the one who stopped along the road and gave them a hand.
They will see every visible manifestation of Christ's life being normally lived out through you.
They will see all that and they "will glorify your Father who is in heaven"

So often when I think of good works they are not the practical, little, daily actions that Chuck mentioned. I think of actions like witnessing, giving tithes and offerings, involvement in some good cause like helping build a house with Habitat for Humanity, being on a church board, teaching a Sunday School class or leading a small group.

It is not that such things are not "good works." We should be involved in things like that, but they are not the twenty-four hours a day, seven days a week "good works" that cause people to take a closer look at us and notice that our heavenly Father is behind what we have been doing.

We have all heard too often of Christians who are religious enough but not Christ-like enough. Movies and books are replete with the caricature of an unloving, self-centered, religious person who is uptight, unloving and

ENCOURAGE

miserable to be around. They push people away from following God. But if our life day in day out is seen to be like the picture Church Swindoll painted, people will be attracted and God will be glorified.

As I looked at each of those actions, I realized that each one is based on our looking not to our own interests but to the interests of others (Phil. 2:4). It is considering others as more important than ourselves. It is seeking the best for others, which is exactly what agape love is all about.

Courtesy to a grumpy salesclerk. A warm smile to a child who bumps into you. A thank you to someone who holds the door for you. An apology to someone for your part of an offense even though their part was much greater. Time and effort given to a person in need even when you don't have much time or energy. I encourage you to let such good works shine, that your Father in heaven may be glorified.

Something to think about before you close this book today:

Look at Swindoll's list of "good works." Check those you do pretty well. Circle those you need to work on a bit more.

Diamonds in the Rough

Many churches on the eastern shore of Maryland and South Carolina, where I was a pastor, had been part of America's early history and have graveyards of overlapping generations. Funeral services in the summer months would be held in the ancient, shaded cemeteries. Often after an internment, I would walk around reading the weathered dates and inscriptions on the worn tombstones--some dating back to the 1700's. Many of the entombed had died in their 20's or 30's--a wife or a child dying from the complications of childbirth. Often there was a grouping of miniature gravestones in a family plot, naming children one, two or three years old. Had a typhoid or cholera epidemic gone through the community? Three hundred years back there were few doctors and medical care was at best primitive.

But as a pastor, I have seen many people face their own trials: troublesome diseases, cancer, malaria and ALS. There have been the recitations of accidents and congenital birth defects, genetic anomalies, depression and many illnesses. For some, there have been persecution and exhaustion from governmental harassment. I have talked with some who have aging parents in need of care, wayward children, troubled marriages, jobs and ministries that don't seem to be productive. There is often a lack of funds and the bitterness of a lost friendship of a colleague.

Has my description of life depressed you? Be happy that things also at times go well: relationships are great, devotional times are meaningful, the weather is glorious, ministry is thriving, the kids are healthy and growing in the Lord and the awesome sunrises are magnificent.

In Ecclesiastes 7:8, King David's son wrote, "Better is the end of a thing than its beginning." Remember that our Lord was a man of sorrows, acquainted with grief, but is now at his Father's right hand, crowned with glory and honor. Remember also, in time "Every knee will bow and every tongue will confess that he is Lord." First the cross, then the crown.

Charles Haddon Spurgeon wrote, "You must bear the cross or you will never wear the crown; you must wade through the water or you will never walk the golden pavement." In his daily devotional book, <u>Morning and Evening</u>, he gave a poetic illustration of a caterpillar, "just a worm crawling in the dirt," which was yet to become a beautiful butterfly, "with gorgeous wings, playing in the sunbeams, sipping at the flowers, full of happiness and life."

It may seem, from time to time, that we are *crawling in the dirt*, but one day when Christ appears we will be like him. Sorrows will become our glory.

Then again, to change the metaphor, Christians are like *diamonds in the rough*. The gifted jeweler knows what that one of a kind rough diamond can become. He carefully, but forthrightly, cuts every facet, then grinds and polishes. The diamond will lose much, much that from the untrained eye seemed important. If the uncut gem could speak, it would complain loudly. "I really don't see why I must go through all this and have my rough edges ground off." But in the end, as the sunlight shines on the multifaceted gem, it will reflect the light-glittering rays of the sun's full spectrum. That never would have been without the cutting and polishing.

We are God's "treasured possession" (Mal. 3:17) and what we face in life is part of the cutting process. Faith and patience will do their perfect work, thus at last, God will hold us in his hand, seeing the glorious spectrum of *His eternal purpose*. "Better is the end of a thing than its beginning."

Something to think about before you close this book today:

You are a diamond in the rough. What are a couple of your "rough edges" that need to be chipped off so that Christ's light can be better reflected to others?

Encouragement in the Midst of Financial Troubles

In 2010 I wrote: No one knows how this present financial crisis will turn out—some have lost jobs and can't find another, savings have support Christian enterprises have lost a third of their portfolios. There is confusion about the future…tension, fear, anxiety for both the non-Christian and the Christian.

But as followers of Christ, whatever crisis we face there are some encouraging truths we can stand on which make a difference in how we face today and the future. First, **God is in charge**; He has, and has always had, a plan and He is not surprised about what happens. He is not caught off guard. He is not in heaven wringing his hands. God is sovereign in all the circumstances of our lives. He always acts with love and grace. He is good.

Note the biblical truths of Isaiah 40.

The nations are like a drop in a bucket; they are regarded as dust on the scales…
God sits enthroned above the earth and its people are like grasshoppers.
He brings princes to naught…
No sooner are they planted…than he blows on them and they wither…
He gives strength to the weary and increases the power of the weak…
those who hope in the Lord will renew their strength.
They will soar on wings like eagles.

Second, we are going to have to **go through** this seeming trial whoever we are--it is not only the investors on Wall Street who will be affected. None of us knows exactly how our economic futures will turn out, but **we will get through**. The promises of God tell us:

I have refined you, though not as silver; I have tested you in the furnace of affliction (Is.48:10).

ENCOURAGE

Can a mother forget the baby at her breast?
Though she may forget, I will not forget you.
See, I have engraved you on the palms of my hands (Is. 49:15).

We will be different people on the other side of any financial crisis. I know I will be.

A couple of good questions to ask ourselves are: What will we like to be like when the downturn is over? What would we like God to do in our lives: spiritually, relationally, morally and financially? Pat Morley, the author of <u>The Man in the Mirror</u> said about the 2008 financial meltdown, "This is my opportunity to show the world there really is a difference being a Christian." As we look at what is happening to our finances and to the security we thought we had, it is easy to be anxious and fearful. But we have another choice. God has promised to never leave us.

Even to your old age and gray hair I am he who will sustain you.
I have made you and I will carry you;
I will sustain you and I will rescue you.   (Is 46:6)

What a great opportunity we have when financial troubles hit to vividly demonstrate to the world that our gospel, our Bible, is true—it sustains us--regardless of circumstances.

Trust in the Lord with all your heart,
lean not on your own understanding,
in all your ways acknowledge him,
and he will make your path straight.
Proverbs 3:5-6

Something to think about before you close this book today:

In the Sermon on the Mount (Matt. 6:25), Jesus said, "Therefore I tell you do not worry about your life, what you will eat or drink; or about your body, what you will wear. Is not the body more that clothes?" What is the last think you worried/fretted about dealing with finances? Talk to Jesus about it. What do you think he will say to you?

Glorifying God When the Storms Hit

I became a Christian at the University of Illinois. Through the providence of God and Inter-Varsity, I came into contact with some outstanding preachers, many of whom were Presbyterian. So as a young follower of Christ I learned the great truth found in the first question of the Westminster Shorter Catechism.

What is the chief end of man?
Man's chief end is to glorify God, and enjoy him forever.

Now, a more mature Christian, one who has been on the road of sanctification for decades, I look at myself and see how far I still have to go. I ask: How can I, how can you and I, glorify God? How can God's glory be manifested through such fallen creatures as we are? As Charles Spurgeon wrote, "We always have a side glance toward our own honor. We have too high an estimate of our own powers and have mixed motives in everything we do." How can we get self out of the way and make room for God to be exalted?

I believe that is the reason why God often brings his people into tough situations or allows them to get into great difficulties. When we become aware of our own folly and weaknesses and then time and again see God work out our deliverance, we begin to see more of the majesty of God.

Spurgeon wrote: "He whose life is one even and smooth path will see but little of the glory of the Lord, for he has few occasions of self-emptying and hence but little fitness for being filled with the revelation of God. They who navigate little streams and shallow creeks know but little of the God of tempests, but they who are 'doing business on the great waters' see 'his wondrous works in the deep.'"

ENCOURAGE

As a pastor, time and again God has made me aware of the grave difficulties and trials that his people go through. And probably many of you right now are navigating much more than "little streams and shallow creeks." Many of you are facing some rough waters and some are facing huge waves. But in those storms that include, financial difficulties, family problems, fellow Christians who attack, needy older parents, wayward children, depression, school decisions, backsliding believers, illness, self-doubt and more, in these we learn the power of our God, because we recognize clearly the littleness of man.

Thank God, then, if you have been or are now sailing on rough seas. It is such that has given and will give you your experience of God's greatness and loving kindness. Spurgeon reminds us that our troubles in the past have enriched us with a wealth of knowledge that can be gained by no other means. Our trials have been and can continue to be the crevice of the rock in which God has set us, as he did Moses, that we might behold his glory as it passes by.

Praise God that you have not been left to the darkness and ignorance that continued prosperity and ease of life might have brought. Know that as you continue to be faithful in the great battle that is the Christian life, you will see more and more of the glory of God as he continues to deal with you in his wonderful way.

Something to think about before you close this book today:
The apostle Paul, who probably faced more trials than we, wrote in II Cor. 4: 8-10, *"We are hard pressed on every side, but not crushed; perplexed, but not in despair; persecuted, but not abandoned; struck down, but not destroyed. We always carry around in our body the death of Jesus, so that the life of Jesus (his resurrection power) may also be revealed in our body."* God is glorified as people see the way we face the storms of life that hit us.

But the glory is not just God's. He graciously lets us be part of it. A few verses later (vv. 16-18) he writes, *"Therefore we do not lose heart. Though outwardly we are wasting away, yet inwardly we are being renewed day by day. For our light and momentary troubles are achieving for us an eternal glory that far outweighs them all. So we do not fix our eyes of what is seen, but on what is unseen. For what is seen is temporal, but what is unseen is eternal."*

ENCOURAGE

God's Surprising Sovereignty

No room for them in the inn." is one of the most poignant phrases in the Christmas story—a story that we retell each year. We imagine, because of their long trip on a donkey, that Joseph was more than worried and frustrated--and certainly both he and Mary were exhausted from their arduous, dusty travel. To climax the event, in Bethlehem there was no place to stay, no room in the inn! He was now also anxious, but Mary was now more concerned than he. Something had to be done...soon.

Then there was our family's story, circa 2004. It certainly was not of the caliber or import of that first Christmas story, but that history changing nativity did compel us to ponder again the meaning of there being *no room.*

We were moving to a new community. Our home was supposedly sold in May and in June. Both sales fell through. *We pondered* what was happening. But we reaffirmed that God is sovereign, so we relaxed. Friends thought we should be a bit more nervous. Since May we had looked for a home in a new community. Nothing we liked or could afford was available. But in July we found a great place to move. But there was the timing of selling, buying and moving that all had to fall into place and instead it fell apart.

The planned sale of our home again fell through a week before closing the end of September. We wondered what God had in mind. Two weeks later there was a third offer. We accepted. But the buyers wanted closing and moving in by the end of October! Oops.

There was *no inn* available in our new city to move into. We needed a home; but our realtor could find nothing. Then a friend who lived there called saying that she had prayed that morning, "Lord, we need to find Joy and Roger a house." Shortly after her amen she saw a house in the late stages of construction. She had seen it week after week as she watch various grandchildren play soccer across the street from it, but had paid no attention. She called us with excitement in her voice, "I found the house you have been praying for." We purchased it three days later. We have been in our new home over a decade and continue to be amazed at how absolutely perfect it is for us.

So why have I gone into this long personal story? Just to remind us all that God is sovereign. He works out His purposes in our lives, works in His time for our good and His glory. It sometimes can feel that we have been forgotten...things fall apart. But we are assured daily that God is sovereign, He is our heavenly Father who delights in doing good things for us.

Sure, Mary and Joseph probably wished for a nice clean inn rather than a damp, smelly stable. It would have been better still if Caesar Augustus had waited a year to tax the world. A trip to Bethlehem was not what they wanted to do in Mary's last stages of pregnancy. But God was working out His glorious purpose even in the midst of the thronging Bethlehem mob and there being no decent place to have a first child--let alone having some rest and a warm meal.

But it is exciting and awesome, every Christmas season, to be reminded that the angels continue to sing *"Glory to God in the highest!"* They unendingly see God's amazing, loving, wise, gracious actions. And every once in a while we also catch a glimpse.

Something to think about before you close this book today:

Take time right now to think about the last time you saw an example of God's amazing sovereignty.

ENCOURAGE

God's Will and Opposition

Joseph took a step of faith when he asked Mary to be his wife. But even then, people all over Nazareth were talking about his betrothed, pregnant but not married. But Joseph still obeyed God no matter what people were saying.

What resulted from his faithful obedience: comfort and ease? No. There was the decree from the Roman government for more taxation. Then came their subsequent, uncomfortable, long trip to Bethlehem where all the inns were full. Obedience led Joseph to major difficulties and discomfort. Add to that a message from God that Herod was trying to kill their young son, so Joseph had to take Jesus and Mary quickly to Egypt.

Spiritual assaults and attacks from the ungodly (and sometimes even friends) are not always signs that we are out of the will of God. They may very well indicate that we are in the center of God's moment for us. Joseph did not face all his hardships because he was cantankerous, but because he was obedient.

In John 15:20 Jesus in essence said to those gathered with him in the upper room: A servant is no greater than the master. Since they persecuted me, naturally they will persecute you. He offered hope when he told the disciples, "In the world *you will have trouble*. But take heart! I have overcome the world."

In his devotional book, Experiencing God: Day by Day, Henry Blackaby reminds us that we should not become discouraged when we face opposition. Opposition from others may indicate that we are centered in our obedience to God. We all need to try not to let opposition cause us to doubt that God is still sovereign and loves us.

When troubles hit, it is easy to think that we are out of God's will. What I do when that happens is to examine my heart and see if I truly believe I am following what He asked. If I am, God will help me move through the tough times and the antagonisms that come. In Acts 4 Peter and John were arrested for obeying God and proclaiming Christ. They did not

ENCOURAGE

ask God to remove the resultant persecutions, but rather asked God to give them boldness as they faced whatever would come.

God's will for you may involve difficulties and opposition. It did for His Son. Likewise, we are promised that He loves us and will never let us face more than we are able to endure.

Be encouraged. Know anew that as we walk with our Lord through this fallen world, He is working out his perfect plan for his glory and our good. Rejoice and be glad!

Something to think about before you close this book today

Remind yourself that Joseph and Mary did not face all those hardships because they were out of God's will, but because they were in the very center of his will. Hold on to that thought the next time troubles hit you.

ENCOURAGE

His Eye is on the Sparrow and I Know He Watches Me

I hope you have heard Ethel Waters sing "His Eye is on the Sparrow." The song starts off: "Why should I feel discouraged? Why should the shadows come? Why should my heart feel lonely?" Those are good questions. Why should we worry and fret? We really don't have to.

If you and I realize how big our God is, it would free us from the anxiety and the fretting we so often live under. God has no difficulty using Satan's plans for his own good purposes. John Calvin was a professor at Paris University. At that time humanist enlightenment scholars had gone back to Greek and Latin manuscripts and looked at the languages in ways that had never been done before. Calvin learned from these humanist scholars so he was able to create Latin and Greek lexicons which proved to be vital as he and others began to translate the Bible into the national languages. We might think that humanism is a work of the devil. In many ways it is, but our great God can even bring good out of it.

We must not forget that the devil is a very subtle enemy. He was too crafty for Adam and Eve in their perfection. How much more dangerous is he to us in our maimed condition. But how good it is to know that the devil may not attack or tempt us unless God allows it. When Jesus went into the wilderness to be tempted, he was led, not by an evil spirit, but by the Holy Spirit (Matt. 4:1). All that transpired was by God's permission. And that same Holy Spirit who led Jesus into the field of battle led him off the field with victory.

When Satan attacks or tempts you or me, he is only serving as God's messenger. Paul called his thorn in the flesh "the messenger of Satan (2 Cor. 12:7). But Paul says that thorn was to keep him humble. The tempter never meant to do Paul such a service, but God let him hit Paul to accomplish his own divine will. The devil and his instruments are both God's instruments.

In 1655 William Gurnall wrote, "The devil and his whole council are mere fools to God...Satan has never been nor will he ever be a worthy opponent of God Almighty. Our Lord so far surpasses the devil in wisdom that He can take the very temptations the enemy uses to batter the saints, and use them instead to build a tabernacle of grace and comfort for His children! ...God wrestles the devil's tools from his own hands and uses them to rebuild what he has been so busily tearing down. Thus God lays, as it were, His own plans under Satan's wings and makes him hatch them. (Remember how He used the evil plot of Joseph's brothers to accomplish His own grand design)."

You may be in the midst of very difficult times right now. You might be facing difficulties or temptations (from the world, the flesh or the devil) that are subtle and strong. But know that God is not so busy wherever the latest earthquake or famine hit that he has forgotten about you.

Never forget that you are very precious to him. The value of something is based on what someone will pay for it. God paid the life of his Son for you so that you might live with him forever. All the things that are hitting you now are but instruments in God's hands that he intends use to conform you to the image of Christ.

Fight the good fight with all thy might!
Christ is thy strength, and Christ thy right;
Lay hold on life, and it shall be
Thy joy and crown eternally.

Something to think about before you close this book today:

Why should I feel discouraged? Why should the shadows come? Why should my heart feel lonely?

ENCOURAGE

How Could I Do Such a Thing?

Recently I read a new printing of an old book: J.C. Ryle's <u>Practical Religion,</u> Evangelical Press, 2001. I highly recommend it.

One chapter spoke to me strongly about two errors I sometimes fall into. Even though I have been a follower of Christ since 1958, I still find my "old nature" coming out too often, more often with those close to me than strangers. I have said more than once, "I would never think of being as ugly to a stranger as I am to my wife." At times I look closely at myself and am ashamed. I think, "How could I do/say/think such a thing? What does God think of me now?"

But Ryle encouraged me here. I hope his words encourage you. He wrote, "The Lord takes pleasure in his believing people. Though stained and spotted in their own eyes, they are beautiful and honorable in his. They are all lovely. He sees 'no spot' in them (Song of Solomon 4:7). Their weaknesses and shortcoming do not break off the union between him and them. He chose them, knowing everything in their hearts. He took them for his own, with a perfect understanding of all their debts, liabilities and weaknesses, and he will never break his covenant and cast them off. When they fall, he will raise them up again. When they wander, he will bring them back. Their prayers are pleasant to him. As a father loves the first stammering efforts of his child to speak, so the Lord loves the poor feeble petitions of his people. He endorses them with his own mighty intercession and gives them power on high. Their acts of service are pleasant to him. As a father delights in the first daisy that his child picks and brings him, so the Lord is pleased with the weak attempts of his people to serve him. Not a single cup of cold water will ever lose its reward. Not a word spoken in love will ever be forgotten. The Holy Spirit inspired the writer of Hebrews to tell of Noah's faith, but not of his drunkenness, of Rahab's faith, but not of her lie."

ENCOURAGE

Wow! That is a good read.

Another thing I do too often is to think of the negative things that come up in life. Ryle reminded me to think more of the privileges I have in Christ. "Peace with God now and glory in the future; the everlasting arms to guide and protect you on your way to heaven and the shelter of safety in the end." I say, yes, but life can be tough. Look at what Christians all over the world are facing. Ryle reminds me, "You say Christians have unique sorrows – you forget they also have unique joys. Just looking at them, you only see half of the Christian life. You do not see everything. You see the warfare but not the daily sustenance and the rewards. You see the struggles and conflicts of the outward part of Christianity but you do not see the hidden treasures that lie deep within. Like Elisha's servant you see the enemies of God's children but you do not, like Elisha, see the chariots and horses of fire that protect them."

Ah, yes, I need to remind myself to set my mind on what is true, what is honorable, what is just, what is pure, what is pleasing and commendable, what is excellent and worthy of praise.

May these thoughts encourage you as you let Christ live his life through you.

Something to think about before you close this book today:

I mentioned how I can get discouraged when I let my old nature come out and when I concentrate on the negatives of living in this fallen world. What causes you to become discouraged? What can you do to more quickly move out of that?

ENCOURAGE

How Not to Grow Weary in Well Doing

Once in Rome I saw Michelangelo's paintings on the Sistine Chapel ceiling. I was amazed that the artist could do that at the advanced age he was. I was also amazed that he could do it up close and it would be in the right perspective for someone looking at it from the floor. Michelangelo created some of the greatest works of art ever. Most of what he painted or sculpted had a religious dimension to it. He was a devout man and took appropriate pride in what he did for God and hoped that his work might help him obtain favor with God. It is so easy to think that what we do for God makes him look on us with a bit more favor.

I read that toward the end of his life, Michelangelo was intrigued with the new Reformed teaching that said we receive God's favor through faith apart from works. He realized that all his good works done for God could not remove his sin and he came to Christ as his forgiving Savior. This changed the meaning of life for him. He recognized that what he had seemingly done for God had actually become more important to him than God. In a sonnet he confessed:

> *Whence the loving fancy that made of art my idol and my king,*
> *I know now well that it was full of wrong.*
> *Painting and sculpture shall no longer calm the soul turned to that love divine that spread its arms on the cross to take us in.*

This new view of his life and work did not cause Michelangelo to stop expressing himself through art. But now he did it for another reason – not for merit but for love. One observer noted, "Michelangelo worked down to the end....Nonetheless the change was a radical one: art which had become the primary interest, the 'idol and king' of his life, now becomes a means to serve God humbly."

We all are children of the Reformers. We do not think of our "good works" as obtaining God's favor. We know Ephesians 2:8-9. But sometimes we may fall into the trap of hoping that our work for God might

ENCOURAGE

cause him to like us a bit more. Or we may fall for a slight different version of that. We do our "good works", our ministry, because we are supposed to and if we don't, what will happen? Or if we work for a Christian organization, we think: We are receiving a salary given by people who are sacrificing to send it to us. If we don't do the work, who will? It's our job.. There is a need out there.

When we let that kind of thinking in, it is so easy to "grow weary in well doing" (2 Thessalonians 3:13). Somehow we get our eyes off what God intended: that all we do is to be an expression of gratitude for his complete favor that we have received because of his grace. The context of that 2 Thessalonians passage has to do with Christians who are not working as they should be. The leaders are told to call such "idle" people to obedience, but they are warned in the process of working for God to not themselves "grow weary in doing good."

If you are a bit weary now, a little miffed at Christians who are not doing what they ought to be doing, not sure if anyone really appreciates what you are doing and what you have sacrificed to serve God as you are, stop and realize that none of that really has anything to do with what you are doing. We are to do our work, our ministry, out of gratitude to God for what he has done for us. He sees your heart. And actually he isn't worried about how much you accomplish for him. Really, he doesn't need us to do things for him. Remember, he doesn't love you more or appreciate you more if you are successful and do more "for him." Faithfulness, not success is the key.

Do what God has called you to do. Seek to do it well. Michelangelo's work wasn't sloppy. Do it as a thank you to God for his amazing love, mercy and grace. Try to keep your eyes on him.

May your "work" for God bless others, God and you.

Something to think about before you close this book today:

Why are you doing "for God" what you are doing...really?

ENCOURAGE

I Just Choose to Be Happy

Having been in ministry for over fifty years, I know there are many different things that hit our lives and discourage us. If you are one who is trying to live for God in this more and more godless culture, you need all the encouragement you can get so the negatives of this world won't get you down and so you can live more positively.

One day at a friend's house I saw a book I had (on purpose) never read, The Power of Positive Thinking, by Norman Vincent Peale. Early in my Christian life I remember people mocking that book and its author saying that he was liberal or didn't really preach the gospel or something like that. "That's why I find Paul appealing and Peale appalling." But for some reason I still decided to read the book. It was very interesting. He certainly didn't express things exactly as I would and did say some things I wouldn't, but he did say a lot about reading the Bible, memorizing it and meditating on it, about faith and about committing ourselves fully to God.

As I read the book I saw in it some biblical truths and patterns of thinking that were helpful to me and I suspect might be to you. They actually weren't new, but rather old truths that I had not thought about recently or rather not put into practice as much as I should.

He described an old man who was once on the Johnny Carson show. He had a happy and radiant personality. His remarks were unpremeditated, naive and very apt. The audience loved him. Johnny asked him what his secret was to happiness. He said he didn't have any great secret. "When I get up in the morning I have two choices—to be happy or unhappy. I just choose to be happy." Peale remarked that though that could be seen as a superficial remark, Abraham Lincoln, who certainly was not superficial, said that people are just about as happy as they make up their minds to be. Later in the chapter Peale recommended that every morning as we arise we should say aloud three times, "This is the day which the Lord has made, I will rejoice and be glad in it" (Psalm 118:24). I need to choose every day to be happy.

That is similar to something my wife taught me. Whenever she begins to feel discouraged or to think negatively, she remembers Philippians 4:8-9, *"Whatever is true, whatever is noble, whatever is right... pure...lovely, admirable, think about such things... and the God of peace will be with you."* She starts thinking of such positive things and through the years has discovered that greatly helps to move from being depressed and negative to being positive and joyful.

Peale also recommended that the last minutes before we fall asleep are a great time to go over memorized scriptures about faith. He said meditating on such verses would modify our thought patterns in a positive way. He wrote, "Saturate your mind with the great words of the Bible. If you will spend one hour a day reading the Bible and committing its passages to memory, allowing them to recondition your personality, the change in you and in your experience will be little short of miraculous." That reminded me of the first Psalm, *"Blessed in the man...whose delight is in the law of the Lord, and on his law he meditates day and night. He is like a tree planted by streams of water...whatever he does prospers."*

He noted several verses from Jesus' teaching we should memorize. Mark 9:23, *"Everything is possible to him who believes."* Matthew 17:20, *"If you have faith, as small as a mustard seed...nothing will be impossible for you."* Matthew 9:29. *"According to your faith it will be done to you."* Peale added, "Believe – believe – so it drives home to you the truth that faith moves mountains." I need to remember that truth.

He also recommended that every morning we pray something like this: "I place this day, my life, my loved ones, my work in the Lord's hands. Whatever happens, whatever results, if I am in the Lord's hands, it is the Lord's will and it is good." I have fallen into the pattern of just assuming since I've given my life to the Lord, it carries on for each day. But I think it would be a good thing for me to do to consciously renew every morning my commitment to God and my trust in him.

One last thought that I needed to be reminded of and perhaps you do too. Peale wrote, "Every day of your life conceive of yourself as living in partnership and companionship with Jesus Christ. If He actually walked by

ENCOURAGE

your side, would you be worried or afraid? Well, then, say to yourself, 'He is with me.' Affirm aloud His promise. 'I am with you always.' Then change it to say. 'He is with me now,' Repeat that affirmation three times every day."

Peale reminded me, "One of the basic truths taught by the Bible is that God is with us. In fact, Christianity begins with that concept, for when Jesus Christ was born He was called Immanuel, meaning 'God with us.' Christianity teaches that in all the difficulties, problems and circumstances of this life, God is close by. We can talk to Him, lean upon Him, get help from Him, and have the inestimable benefit of His interest, support and help."

What a simple truth, but I so often forget. Christ *is* walking with me right now. So why should I ever fret and worry? Philippians 4:6, *"Do not be anxious about anything, but in everything, by prayer and petition, with thanksgiving, present your requests to God, and the peace of God...will guard your hearts and your minds in Christ Jesus."*

Something to think about before you close this book today:

I mentioned above four things we can do to live daily more positively for Christ. List the four here. Which one do you think could be most important for you? Decide to do it starting today. Tell someone to check now and then on how you are doing. Write that person's name here.

_____

1.

2.

3.

4.

Why Did You Doubt?

Jesus walked on water. But why didn't he just walk around the lake and catch up with the disciples when they landed? One guess is that it was an opportunity for him to build his disciples' faith, to help them better see who he really was.

Did Jesus' miracle accomplish that? Matthew recorded that after Jesus got into the boat the disciples worshiped Him and affirmed that he *truly was* the Son of God. But in the midst of that cataclysmic event, there was one who learned more about Jesus and faith than the others. Remarkable, impulsive Peter called out to Jesus, who was standing in the middle of the stormy lake, "Tell me to come to you by walking on the water." Why would he ask *that*? Perhaps pride and impetuousness. If that were true, I don't think Jesus would have said, *"Come."*

John Ortburg, in <u>If You Want to Walk on the Water, You have to Get Out of the Boat,</u> has written that he thinks Peter had a sudden insight into what Jesus was doing *"The Lord is passing by. He's inviting Peter to go on the adventure of his life."* Peter knows he can stay in the safety and security of the boat, or he can accept Jesus' invitation: Come, step over the side of the boat and join me in what I am doing.

Peter scrambled over the side of the boat and took probably five or six steps. He was dazzled that he didn't sink. Incredible! No one he knew had ever done *that* before. Jesus smiled. But Peter did what we too often do--especially when we are over our heads responding to what God has called us to do.

Peter's problem was that he began to look only at the problems, the huge waves, the crashes of thunder, ferocious lightening, and in so doing took his eyes off Jesus. "I'm sinking!"

ENCOURAGE

Was Jesus surprised by Peter's "failure" and terror? No. When Peter cried out, "I'm sinking. I'm going to drown. I don't know how to swim!" Jesus quietly reached out to him. He gently asked, *Why did you doubt?* He made no attempt to scold or embarrass Peter before the others. He wasn't harsh or critical.

A few of the things I have tried to do for Christ did not turn out very well—actually, more than a few. I've sunk more than once. I doubt that my motives have ever been pure. But Christ continues to encourage me to *step out of the boat*—regardless of the potential danger. At times I take a few steps and that is always exciting. Other times I quickly start to sink, but his hand is always there and his smile and his gentle rebuke: *Friend, you didn't need to doubt. Get yourself dry and get ready for the next adventure I have for you.*

I'm looking forward the next time to maybe taking eight or nine steps.

Something to think about before you close this book today:

What is the next adventure you think Jesus may be calling you to? Don't forget to keep your eyes on Jesus and not the problems.

Especially Need Encouragement?

I've joked at times saying that probably we shouldn't ever vote in a presidential election because a person would have to be crazy to want to be president and we shouldn't vote for a crazy person. Now you don't have to be crazy to run for president, but how hard it would be to have everything you do examined in detail, have your motives questioned and your words twisted. But actually that is what happens in part to anyone in a leadership position.

At the 2004 Republican Convention President Bush said, *"One thing I've learned about the presidency is that whatever shortcomings you have, people are going to notice them and whatever strengths you have, you're going to need them."*

Those words immediately caught my attention because I've experienced that very thing. I would suspect most of you have too because many of you are in some position of leadership. When we blow it in some way, people will quickly point it out and seem to delight in doing so. Because we all have shortcomings and we don't do everything perfectly and don't do everything to please everyone, it can get discouraging to be talked about negatively.

When God calls us to step out in leadership, it is a great privilege, but also we need to recognize that there are negatives to being in a position of leadership. We'll experience a variety of problems. Some of the problems will be just because things go wrong in this fallen world: people let us down, computers crash, hurricanes come, flights get cancelled, etc. Other stresses are caused by people who now look at us differently because we are leading, who disagree with what we are doing and question why we are doing it that way.

So, should no one run for president or should we never let ourselves get into a position of leadership? No, but we should remember that the second we stick our head up, it is likely that someone will shoot at it. Years ago I listened to a series of tapes on leadership. The speaker was Howard Hendricks. He surprised me by saying that the most important quality a leader needed was perseverance. I didn't really understand that at first, but now years later I realize he was right.

The dictionary defines persevere as: *to continue in an undertaking in spite of counter influences, opposition, or discouragement.* I think that is why the imperative *encourage* is used fourteen times in the epistles and why Paul tells Timothy, *"Watch your life and doctrine closely.* Persevere *in them, because if you do, you will save both yourself and your hearers."* And why the writer to the Hebrews after speaking of the suffering they had received tells them (10:35-36) *"So do not throw away your confidence; it will be richly rewarded. [36] You need to* persevere *so that when you have done the will of God, you will receive what he has promised."*

So, if right now because God has placed you in a position of leadership in some area of life (home, work, church) you are facing a difficult situation or a difficult person, remember that God called you to be that leader there and as you turn to him he will by his Holy Spirit encourage you, be your *comforter (cum fortis-to come with strength)*, so that you might persevere, that is: *to continue in an undertaking in spite of counter influences, opposition, or discouragement.*

Another aspect of this is if you recognize that someone else is going through a tough time, be an encourager to them. Enough people are probably already pointing out their shortcomings.

Some things to ask yourself before you close this book today:

Where today do you need to persevere?

Whom might you encourage today?

What Life Are You Waiting For?

A number of years ago Joni Eareckson Tada during a Q and A session following one of her talks, was asked how she kept going--in spite of the challenge of being quadriplegic. She answered, "This is the only time in history when I get to fight for God. This is the only part of my eternal story when I am actually in the battle. Once I die, I'll be in celebration mode in a glorified body in a whole different set of circumstances. But this is my limited window of opportunity, and I'm going to fight the good fight for all I'm worth."

I need to remind myself of that truth because at times I find it hard *to keep at it*. There have been times when I have been discouraged, times when the opposition has been strong, times when I have been tired. It's then that I remember Bill Hybels' quote, "If I am waiting for some other life to be courageous, then I'm kidding myself."

Hybels' words help me realize that, as far as I can tell, only during these short years on this earth can I fight for righteousness, speak to those who do not know the Savior, teach disciples to trust Him and seek to push back the evil that is so aggressive. Only now can I honor our Lord in the middle of this fallen world and put on the whole armor of God and, by faith, step into the battle trusting God's promises.

Do you, like I, ever get tired of the battle? Do you at times want to relax and just take it easy?

Once a member of a church I was pastoring wrote a thirty-nine-page letter to the elders telling them what a *poor* pastor I was. Naturally, I was wounded. Happily, it helped a bit when I heard that the same disgruntled man had gotten 400 church members to vote *no confidence* for a previous pastor. But still, my moment of scorn was not easy for me.

ENCOURAGE

In critical moments, like those harsh comments from an angry man, I had to remind my wounded self that, I was not perfect (and couldn't be) and God, *knowing my imperfections* had still called me to be a soldier in His army. That moment of years ago criticism was not a time to step back and lick my wounds. So I asked myself: *Roger, what life are you waiting for?* As Hybels wrote, "This isn't some pre-game warm-up. It's the *game*, and the clock is ticking."

What life are *you* waiting for?

Something to ask yourself before you close this book today:

Read again Joni's answer to the question of how she keeps going. How would you answer that question?

ENCOURAGE

Living the Hidden Life

Have you, like I, ever thought, "I want to be more like Jesus?"

But as we muse on that thought, sometimes we don't see many results from all our labors for the Lord. We look at a typical day or week which is taken up with wearying and mundane business. It always takes a long time to get our aging car fixed; then working out the insurance for that little dent. Then it takes time getting the kids ready for school. Did we remember to keep good financial records and work on the nagging income tax report. Hurry, hurry. It all takes more time than we ever imagined. Then that head cold had us in bed for half the week. Then, "I'll just take a quick run to the grocery store" and that takes half the day because I decided to take a moment to shop for my mom's birthday. There went the whole morning.

Will we ever have time for ministry? When we get to heaven will we hear, "Well done, good and faithful servant. Enter into the joy of your Master."? Maybe not, we worry.

But think about it for a moment. The largest part of Jesus' life was *not ministry* as we like to think of the term. Rather he lived thirty years in his parents' Nazareth home. Then speculate, he probably spent ten to twelve hours a day working often alone, designing, sawing, gluing and pegging works in wood. Unfortunately, we typically think about Jesus only teaching and creating dazzling miracles.

But we should never forget that, before the spectacular ministry, he lived a simple, quiet life in a small town, far away from great people, great cities or significant events. As Henri Nouwen wrote, "Jesus' hidden life is very important for our own spiritual journeys." We not only need to follow Jesus with our words and deeds of service, but learn to follow him in the

ENCOURAGE

simple, unspectacular and ordinary parts of our life. That is what most of our lives are all about.

Sure, there are the wonderful times of direct ministry, but the trap we so easily fall into causes us to wants to see instant results from our work. We want to feel productive and see what *we* have accomplished. But this is often not the way with the Kingdom of God. It is wonderful when our work for God results in instant, tangible results, but often that is not what happens. If you think about it, Jesus didn't have a lot of tangible results. He died, as his world thought, as a failure, executed as a criminal by the government. If most people of his day looked at his life, they would have thought--if they thought at all--that he died without accomplishing very much.

Jesus' fruitfulness was not what the world thinks of as success. But he did all that the Father had for him to do. As faithful servants of Jesus, we have to trust that our lives too will be fruitful even though we cannot see daily results. Very often the fruit of our lives will only be seen years later. *Sometimes* a person's fruit *is* seen quickly, but we should not envy them or knock ourselves. Our job is to be faithful and loving. God will make our efforts and love fruitful, whether we see this or not.

Something to ask yourself before you close this book today:

What changes do you need to make so that you follow Jesus better in those simple, unspectacular, ordinary parts of your life?

ENCOURAGE

Looking Not Just to Our Own Interests

In a small group discussion recently, I heard a friend say something like this: "Jesus is spoken of as fulfilling three roles: prophet, priest and king." I thought about the Bible speaking of us being daily conformed to the image of Christ. I think that includes our roles as prophet, priest and king. Now I don't mind being in the role of king in our home. I like having my way, telling people what to do and being in charge. I also don't mind being the prophet and letting "my will" be known and stating what I think is the "right" way of doing things. But the role of priest...that is something different. I am not quite so quick in sacrificing myself for others or putting my wife's ways of doing things above mine, or serving her by putting her desires above mine. I don't really feel for others as I feel for myself.

Even being a follower of Christ now for over 50 years, it is still hard for me to follow Philippians 2. *"Do nothing from selfish ambition or vain conceit, but in humility regard others as better than yourselves. Let each of you look not to your own interests but also to the interests of others. Let the same mind be in you that was in Christ Jesus."*

I could fairly quickly get myself in a funk if I just looked at myself and how far short I fall from Christ likeness. One thing that helps me a bit is something I once heard. *I'm not what I should be. I'm not what I want to be. I'm not what I am going to be, but, thank God, I am not what I used to be.*

What helps me even more is to think about what really happened at the Incarnation. The Son of God, the one through whom the whole universe was created, the infinite, eternal God, did not hold on to his rightful position and privileges but, for me, came to my world as a helpless little baby. He gave up so much for me to do that. He took on all kinds of hardship and suffering because of his love. It wasn't because I deserved to be so treated

ENCOURAGE

or that I was so special that it was incumbent upon him to do all this for me. It was because of his love.

Slow down a few minutes and one morning during your devotions, take some time to think of what Jesus left to become a helpless baby, to be born of poor parents in a strange village where there was no room in the inn and he had to be placed in an animal's feeding trough for a cradle. And think about the fact that he did that because he loves you and wanted to make it possible for you to be with him forever.

Thirty-three years later our great High Priest gave himself as the sacrifice for our sins, but long before that he showed us what it was like to *"look not only to your own interests but also to the interests of others."* I think if we see more clearly what Jesus sacrificed for us when he came to our world, we will find it easier to show our gratitude to him by giving to others, especially in our own household, the kind of love he gave to us.

"You have given so much to me; give me one more thing, a grateful heart." George Herbert

Something to ask yourself before you close this book today:

When you take time to think about what Jesus left to come to earth and what it cost him so he could do for you what you could not do for yourself, what comes to your mind as to how you can tell him, "Thank you"?

ENCOURAGE

On Breaking Bruised Reeds

A number of years ago a traveling choir performed at our church. The members of the choir were young men with Down's syndrome who lived in a residence for men and women.

Five of the traveling group stayed overnight at our home. The leader of the five was a delightful and caring young man. We treated the young men to ice cream. It was impressive to see their delight at getting a treat and how they helped one another order a favorite flavor, and then clean up the tables afterwards.

Sam, one of the young men, asked if, in the morning he could prepare breakfast for everyone. "Breakfast is my specialty," he confidently boasted.

What if he were to forget something on the stove or scorches a pan? I worried. Of course I wanted to encourage Sam as much as I could, so I said, "Sure, fix us all a great breakfast. Joy and I will help, if you want." It was a wonderful breakfast! The cook was thrilled to be able serve everyone. He basked in the praise.

Sure, it was a bit risky to open our home and kitchen to five unknown guys with Downs.

However, while breakfast was being cooked, Howard decided he wanted to take a bath. He mistakenly let the water fill the tub then run over. The sudsy water leaked into the pantry and kitchen below. In spite of the small mishap it was great to see how the other young men helped get everything cleaned up, and especially how gently and lovingly they treated their friend who had made the mistake. They took mistakes in stride and worked together to solve them.

That experience helped me better understand what Matthew meant when he quoted Isaiah to describe Jesus:

ENCOURAGE

"A bruised reed he will not break, and a smoldering wick he will not snuff out."

In our throw-away-world we too frequently take that which is slightly damaged and toss it out. We don't have time to fix it, so out it goes. "I don't have time for her anymore, she's divorced." "He just drinks too much, then drives his car." "They don't discipline their kids at all." "She's always depressed." "He's got a terrible temper." "He *blew it* with his dumb business decisions."

Henri Nouwen wrote, "When we dismiss people out of hand because of their apparent woundedness, we stunt their lives by ignoring their gifts which are often buried in their wounds."

Jesus does not ignore *our woundedness* nor dismiss us. He does not think we are worthless because we are damaged. In fact, our shared weaknesses are often the greatest gift we have to give to those around us. Strength is hidden in weakness and as Nouwen said, "True community is a fellowship of the weak."

Genuine Christian fellowship is not a talent show in which we attempt to dazzle one another with our gifts. Even though we may live in a Christian community, we remain challenged to deal with one another as Jesus would deal with us. He does not break the bruised reed nor quench the smallest hope. Surprisingly our strengths can be hidden in our weaknesses.

I discovered I needn't look at our five young guests as handicapped or limited, but rather as caring, warm, generous brothers in Christ from whom I could learn a great deal.

Jerry Kirk, a pastor in Cincinnati, told a group of young pastors, "The greatest gift we have to give to our congregation is our weaknesses." Over the years I have discovered how right he was.

Something to ask yourself before you close this book today: What did Nouwen mean when he said, "True community is a fellowship of the weak?"

I'm Working Hard. Why Don't Things Work Out?

Do you ever wonder why at times it seems that nothing is working out? Your best efforts produce no positive results and your prayers seem to go unanswered and at other times it is just the opposite? I do.

But then I'm reminded of when Jesus, along with Peter, James and John came down from the mountain where they had just seen Jesus dramatically and dazzlingly transformed before them. When they reached level ground, a man with came up and said,

"Teacher, I brought my son for you to heal him. He can't speak because he is possessed by an evil spirit that won't let him talk. And whenever this evil spirit seizes him, it throws him violently to the ground and makes him foam at the mouth and grind his teeth and become rigid. So I asked your disciple to drive out the evil spirit, but they couldn't do it." (NLT)

The other day when I was rereading that story I began to wonder why the disciples couldn't cast out the demon, since Jesus had already commissioned them to do so and earlier they had been successful. Mark wrote *...they cast out many demons and healed many sick people."*

Kent Hughes, former pastor of Wheaton College Church, noted that the disciples' failure in this case was not because they didn't try. They did their best. They did what they had done before and been successful. Jesus said the reason they couldn't cast out the demon was because of unbelief. *"Oh unbelieving generation...how long shall I stay with you."* What unbelief? They believed in their method. It had worked before. They believed in themselves. They had cast out many demons before. What had happened? I'm sure they wondered what they did not believe.

So, sure enough, as soon as Jesus and his men were alone they asked him, *"Why couldn't we drive out the demon?"* Jesus said: *"Prayer."* Hughes helped me to remember what had really happened. "During those six days that Jesus was gone, the disciples had gone about their work, preaching and casting out evil spirits as usual. When they came to the particularly stubborn demon in the boy, they tried and failed. ...nothing worked. Why? Because they somehow began to think that the gift they had received for exorcism was under their control and could be exercised at will."

They didn't think to pray! They forgot about the need of a radical dependence on God's power. *Jesus was teaching them that the faith which brings power is a faith that prays.* The demon would have been history if the disciples had first given themselves to believing prayer.

Have you, like me, ever fallen into that trap? We become involved in a ministry that is way over our heads. We ask Jesus for help, wisdom and power. And we receive them. And God does amazing things through us. Then as time goes by we minister as usual, but our eyes are not on Jesus as before. We don't pray as we first did. And though we have faith in the successful way we have been doing things, we are not resting our faith in Him. We do not desperately go to Jesus in faith and prayer.

When one believes that Jesus is who he claimed to be, that the transfiguration showed what he is really like, ...*this is my Son whom I love*... then we believe in a Christ who fulfills his word to us. When we believe this, our lives will be given more and more to *dependent* prayer. There will be renewed power in our lives to do the ministry God has given us.

The purpose of the Prayer Task Force of the mission I work with is to: *undergird and empower the ministry of the mission with strategic and organized prayer*. Notice the word "empower." Prayer is the key to that.

The disciples worked hard for Jesus, but often they failed to accomplish much. Hard work is not the key. Faithful prayer is. May we learn from their experience and become women and men of believing, effective prayer.

Something to ask yourself before you close this book today: Is there anything that you are involved in now where you see yourself acting like the disciples when they couldn't cast out the demon? Take time to talk to God about what is going on?

ENCOURAGE

Protecting Our Children from God

I love to visit our daughter, son-in-law and our two grandsons. Like all indulgent grandparents we have enjoyed being with and playing with them We bike around the area, work out at the local gym, go into Chicago and just generally have a great time. But one visit, I'm sad to report, I had a humdinger of a bicycle accident: inadvertently I went over my handlebars and met the ground with my nose and head. (Don't ask about the embarrassing details.) Happily the x-rays showed no broken neck, the CAT scan, much to my surprise, showed that I had an unharmed brain--though obviously I hadn't used it well on that bike. For weeks my neck was painfully complaining, "Don't do that AGAIN!"

Being unable to do much else, I had a refreshing time reading. I guess Romans 8:28 still applies today.

The first book I read was an autobiography by John Paton, a missionary to the New Hebrides during the last half of the 1800's. Earlier generations knew Paton's story well. I and probably most of you have barely heard of him. When I started, I never suspected that after a few chapters and a bucket of tears, I would conclude that it was the best missionary biography I had ever read. I heartily recommend it. *

Let me share just a couple things I picked up from my reading.

When John felt led to go to the New Hebrides, everyone was against his going, for he had built an effective inner-city ministry in Glasgow, Scotland, and people didn't want to lose his leadership there. (Ever heard anything like that before?) His parents characteristically counseled that "they had long since given me away to the Lord, and in this matter also would leave me to God's disposal." All of his friends continued to oppose his going to the New Hebrides. One old Christian gentleman's crowning argument was, "You will be eaten by cannibals." Paton replied, "Mr. Avery, you will soon be in the grave and eaten by worms. I confess to

119

ENCOURAGE

you that if I can but live and die serving and honoring the Lord Jesus, it will make no difference to me whether I am eaten by cannibals *or* by worms."

Upon meeting with so many objections to his plans, he again laid the whole matter before his parents who surprised him by replying, "Heretofore we feared to bias you, but now we must tell you how we praise God for the decision to which you have been led. Your father's heart was set upon being a minister, but other claims forced him to give it up. When you were given to us, we laid you upon the altar, our first-born, to be consecrated, if God saw fit, as a Missionary of the Cross--and it has been our constant prayer that you might be prepared, qualified; and led to this very decision; and we pray with all our hearts that the Lord may accept your offering, long spare you and give you many souls from the heathen world for your hire."

Oh, how we need this attitude toward our children.

Over the years I have seen Christian parents sacrificially serving the Lord, but when it came to their children, they wanted them to be *successful* and have *a better life* than they had had: an influential career, wealth, a big house.

May we be more like John Paton's parents and give our children fully to the Lord and not try to "protect" them from decisions that would lead them into a dangerous career or, from the world's point of view, a career that would never get them the *good things* of life.

We never need to "protect" our children from God.

It is interesting that God did answer Paton's parents' prayers. God did accept his offering, long spared him and gave him many souls for his hire. In addition, God used John Paton as the instrument to call many to their own missionary work.

May the prayers for our children and grandchildren be like Paton's parents' prayers. May we, with all our heart, freely consecrate them to God for His good service.

And, oh yes, my aching neck and facial scrapes and embarrassed ego healed nicely, thank you very much.

ENCOURAGE

* <u>Missionary Patriarch, The True Story of John Paton,</u> Vision Forum, 2002-2006

Something to do just after you close this book today:

Go to AMAZON.COM and order the book ($9.99 or less if used). If you truly can't afford it, email me and I'll order one for you.

ENCOURAGE

The Church of Jesus Christ Is On the Move

The growth of the Church of Jesus Christ worldwide has greatly encouraged me. I thought I would pass some of the facts on to you so we might rejoice together in what God is doing these last days.

The data is from research done by Dr. Steve Steele who had been the longtime president of DAWN (Discipling A Whole Nation).

I thought I had kept up pretty well with what Christ's Church is doing around the world, but reading this research, I realize that my knowledge is several years behind. That wouldn't be too far behind except for the fact that in these last years the Church worldwide has expanded as never before in history. I was stunned to read Steve's report. I could hardly believe it. But in talking with him, I discovered that the statistics are from forty or so networks worldwide that he has contact with. He said there are networks he doesn't know about, so, in reality, the numbers would actually be greater than what he has.

India has 1/6 or more of the world's population. God has chosen to work in that giant country as never before. In 2001 the census of India estimated 2.1% Christians. In January 2005 the government estimated 6.8%. In those four years forty million Hindus became Christians. That is 27,400 per day! Over 100,000 churches were started in 2005. A few years ago few young Indian Christian men or women volunteered to be trained to go out and plant churches. But then God moved and they began to. For example Victor Choudrie was a cancer surgeon in London. God called him to move back to India. He burned his passport and has started 70,000 churches so far!

What Has God done to make India so open? He has used a number of factors that have helped Church growth. I'll mention just a few.

ENCOURAGE

1. In the 2004 national elections the more radical Hindu party, the BJP, was expected to win as they had always done. Four million Christians fasted and prayed for the election and to everyone's surprise the more moderate, secular Congress party won. One principle for their governance states "To preserve, protect and promote social harmony and to enforce the law without fear or favour to deal with all fundamentalist elements who seek to disturb social amity and peace." Though there are still places where Christians are persecuted, it is now less in some locations.

2. The Dalit (untouchable) community and the lower castes (250 million people, 1/4 of the population) have been oppressed for 3000 years by the Hindu caste system. Their leaders decided to lead their people to join a "foreign" religion, meaning: Islam, Buddhism or Christianity. They hate the Muslims; there are few Buddhist priests or temples in India, and Christianity gives them a dignity Hinduism never could – the right to be called sons and daughters of God. There has been a massive people movement toward Christianity among the Dalits.

3. In 2001 the festival of Kumbha Mela was held. This only happens every 144 years. It is based on Indian mythology as the time when Hindus can have their sins washed away. Seventy million Hindus went to the three rivers as pilgrims, but they came out feeling as before. Christ followers were there and sold 40 million pieces of Christian literature. Also if you did not have your sins washed away there, you will have to wait till the year 2145. Many are now more open to looking at other options for hope and assurance.

4. Several years ago an Australian missionary, Graham Stain, and his two boys were stopped by a radical Hindu mob. They were butchered, their bodies thrown into their car and it was burned. Moderate Hindus were embarrassed by this. Then on TV Graham's widow was interviewed and she spoke of forgiving those who had done this. This impacted Hindus who know little of such forgiveness.

China has 1.35 billion people. The church is growing as never before. Dr. Steele said they have less empirical research on China, but estimate there are over 20 million new believers a year. It is estimated that there are 130 million Christians in China. There are over 1000 house churches in Beijing alone. Because the 2008 Olympics were held there, the government created a massive program to teach English before the

Olympics. It is estimated by the government that 300 million people will move from the countryside to the cities. Ken Wendling, founder of ELIC (English Language Institute of China), said that four out of five of such transients are open to Christianity.

There are also wonderful things taking place in the Islamic world and in Latin America. In Uzbekistan in 1990 there were less than ten known Uzbek believers. In 2008 the mission I work with had contact with over 5000. It is estimated that there are over 500,000 believers in Mongolia.

Largely because of the oppression of the fundamentalist mullahs in Iran, many people are looking at Christianity. Tens of thousands have come to faith in Christ.

I hope this encourages you. The United States and Europe are basically the only places in the world where the church is stagnant or shrinking. It is easy for us to be a bit discouraged, but don't be. God has called you to live where you are and he is working out his perfect will in and through your life. The Church of Jesus Christ is not dying or stagnant. It is expanding as never before. You are called to be part of that.

Something to think about before you close this book today:

People in transition, having moved from their country, are more open to looking at Christianity. Look around and see if there are internationals or refugees you can reach out to.

The Kingdom of God and Hardships

>Psalm 16:5-6 (NIV)
>Lord, you have assigned me my portion and my cup;
>you have made my lot secure.
>The boundary lines have fallen for
>me in pleasant places;
>surely I have a delightful inheritance.

Most of you who are reading this could say that these verses fit your lives. Yet God's people have their trials. We have seen this all through history and we know it by experience.

In Lystra Paul was first acclaimed as a god and a short time later was stoned and thought dead. Afterwards it says in Acts 14:22 that he returned to Lystra strengthening the disciples and encouraging them to remain true to the faith. He said "We must go through many hardships to enter the kingdom of God." That is almost a promise. In this fallen world, God's people will "go through many hardships."

Spurgeon said, "It was never God's plan, when He chose His people, that they should be untested. They were chosen in the furnace of affliction; they were never chosen for worldly peace and earthly joy."

What is good to know is that it is our loving heavenly Father who has ordained the season and place, the intensity and the effect of the trials we will face. Spurgeon added, "Good men (and women) must never expect to escape troubles; it they do, they will be disappointed for none of their predecessors have been without them."

I remember early in my Christian life when I first read the Old Testament how surprised I was to see God's men and women so often getting clobbered. Then I began to read biographies of missionaries. Whoa!

As they gave themselves to serve God, they were not at all excused from the troubles of life. Spurgeon agreed, "Each of those whom God made vessels of mercy were made to pass through the fire of affliction."

It is true that compared with most people living in the Darfur region of Sudan, North Korea, the rural areas of China or India, the slums of Nairobi and many other cities, and actually most people in the world, most of us can say that "the lines have fallen for us in pleasant places." But just comparing our trials with those of others does not give us much help in facing the tough times that come.

What does help? We have the comfort of knowing that our Master has walked that path before us. We also have "his presence and sympathy to cheer us, his grace to support us and his example to teach us how to endure" (Spurgeon). And we have something else that makes all the difference. When we reach "the kingdom" it will more than make amends for the "many tribulations" through which we have passed to enter it.

Something to ask yourself before you close this book today:

What do you find helpful when troubles hit? Look again at what Spurgeon said in the last paragraph. Which of his thoughts are the most meaningful to you?

ENCOURAGE

Trusting that God Is Good

Margaret Paton and her husband, John worked with the cannibals of the New Hebrides during the 1860's-90's. She was a candid, positive, humorous person and her once-a-year letters were a delight to read. As I read her book, which was a compilation of these letters, some of the stories she related made me laugh out loud. However, sometimes they described such incredibly painful experiences that I had to stop reading. I couldn't see the page because of the tears in my eyes. They lost two of their children to disease. She described poignantly the intense loneliness she felt when her children were away in Australia for schooling and John was also gone for months and she was the only white person on the island. There was great disappointment when a native girl she had spent much time with and who seemed so promising turned from Christ and went back to the old ways.

At times I sensed a little questioning of God on her part, but it was quickly put behind her. Her faith and trust in God overcame all obstacles. The last chapter was written by one of her sons and it describes her death. I had fully expected that she would die in her sleep or in her chair with the Bible on her lap. That didn't happen. She got a painful cancer and in her last year she fought pain every day, not letting anyone know. Her last six weeks the pain grew fiercer. And on 16 May 1905 in her sleep she died.

When I read the last chapter of her book, at first I was a bit sad/upset that God had this wonderful, godly woman go through such a painful end. In my mind I knew that God does all things perfectly, but still wondered why didn't she have one of those wonderful, gentle home goings.

In the providence of God, the next morning's reading from Spurgeon's daily devotional, <u>Morning and Evening</u>, spoke to my questions. God reminded me how I should look at such things. Spurgeon was commenting on Amos 9:9 where God says he will sift Israel, but not the smallest, lightest, shriveled grain will fall to the ground, just the chaff. He wrote, "Every sifting comes by divine command and permission. Satan must ask permission before he can lay a finger upon Job. In actual fact, in some sense our siftings are directly the work of heaven...Satan may hold the sieve, hoping for the worst, but the overruling hand of the Master is accomplishing His purpose by the very process that the enemy hopes will be destructive. Precious child of God, even though you are shaken, be comforted by the blessed fact that the Lord directs the whole process for His own glory and for your eternal profit."

I went back to an earlier of Spurgeon's devotions on a similar topic. He wrote, "Yesterday I could climb the mountain and ...rejoice with confidence in my future inheritance; today my spirit has no hopes, but many fears, no joys, but great distress. Is this a part of God's plan for me? ...

"Yes, it is even so. The eclipse of your faith, the darkness of your mind, the fainting of your hope—all these things are just parts of God's method of making you ready for the great inheritance, which you will soon enjoy. The trials are for the testing and strengthening of your faith. ...Do not think, believer, that your sorrows are out of God's plan; they are necessary parts of it. 'Through many tribulations we must enter the kingdom,' Learn, then, to 'count it all joy...when you meet trails of various kinds.'"

O let my trembling soul be still, and trust Thy wise, Thy holy will!

I cannot, Lord, Thy purpose see, yet all is well since ruled by Thee.

Something to do before you close this book today:

Write down below something in today's reading that you found helpful.

ENCOURAGE

Ugly Brown Stains

Paul, Silas and Timothy glowingly wrote (I Thessalonians 4) about what will take place at Christ's breathtakingly spectacular return – trumpets, archangels, resurrections, the new heaven and new earth! He then says: *"So comfort and encourage each other with these words."*

Since we live and work in a fallen and twisted world--at once beautifully awesome, yet distorted and broken by our sin, the Bible says that soon it is God's intention to put it all right. So in the midst of our contemporary pain and troubles, we can joyously look forward to newly restored bodies, attitudes and relationships where we can live without anguish, disappointment or betrayal in a new heaven and earth.

In the meantime you or a loved one may be experiencing sorrow and sufferings that overwhelm. You may be nagged by guilt or dismaying memories. Happily we can be reassured that one day He will *wipe away every tear from our eyes. There will be no more death or mourning or crying or pain.*

Even now God gives us encouragement—even when it's difficult to accept. My favorite reassurance is when Paul scribes a note to the Romans *"in all things God works for the good of those who love him"* (Romans 8:28).

Anne Graham Lotz wrote in <u>Heaven: My Father's House.</u>

A group of fishermen sitting around a table in a small pub were telling their "fish stories." As one of the men flung out his arms to more vividly describe the fish that got way, he accidentally hit the tray of drinks that the young barmaid was bringing to the table. The tray and the drinks sailed thought the air, crash-landing against the newly whitewashed wall. As the sound of smashed glass and splashing beer permeated the room, the pub became silent as all eyes turned to the ugly brown stain that was forming on the wall.

ENCOURAGE

Before anyone could recover from the startling interruption, a guest who had been sitting quietly by himself in the corner jumped up, pulling a piece of charcoal from his pocket and began to quickly sketch around the ugly brown stain. To the amazement of everyone present, right before their eyes the stain was transformed into a magnificent stag with antlers outstretched, racing across a highland meadow. Then the guest signed his impromptu work of art. His name was Sir Edwin Landseer, Great Britain's foremost wildlife artist.

God transforms our lives as Sir Landseer transformed the mindless, accidental smear on the pub wall. Whatever ugly brown stains we bear, God promises us that He will transform them for good. Lotz assures us that, "God excels in transforming ugly brown stains into beauty marks when we surrender them to Him. He will bring peace and freedom to you and glory to Himself."

God's good world tragically has been distorted by the effects of our blatant, purposeful or naive sins. But the Bible says that God is not going to throw away his handiwork and start from scratch. Instead He is going to use our same old mottled canvas on which He will repair and make more beautiful the painting that has been marred by the evil one. As one writer said, "The vandal doesn't get the satisfaction of destroying his rival's masterpiece. On the contrary God, the impeccable creator, intends to create an even greater masterpiece out of what the enemy sought to destroy." God will use everything that comes into our lives, so that one day we will thank him for everything – even the ugly brown stains.

When we get to heaven, hallelujah, there won't be any scars, no suffering of any kind, including the kind that has impacted or is impacting our lives right now. *Be encouraged*!

Something to do before you close this book today:

Take a minute and try to think of a time when Romans 8:28 was true for you. Then thank God that he will always work all things for the good to those who love him.

When Troubles Come

God miraculously provided food for the Israelites in their wilderness journey. Did the Israelites thank God for that? No, they romanticized their past in Egypt, minimizing the troubles there and bitterly complained to Moses about the manna God was providing. So Moses went to the Lord and asked, "Why have you brought this trouble on your servant. What have I done to displease you...?" (Numbers 11:11)

We've not exactly been in the same situation, but I know I have asked the Lord that same question: Why have you brought this trouble on your servant? Sometimes I've even gotten introspective and added the thought: Is it because I did such and such or didn't do such and such? Am I being punished for that?

That kind of thinking can get pretty morbid and usually gets me nowhere. I've discovered that if I am being disobedient, the Holy Spirit has more effective ways of showing me that than putting me through troubles.

It is true that sometimes we bring troubles upon ourselves, but it is also true that our heavenly Father at times does send us troubles. I read of three reasons he does that.

First, troubles test our faith. If it is true faith, it will stand the test. Spurgeon wrote, "Gilt is afraid of fire, but gold is not. The imitation gem dreads being touched by the diamond, but the true jewel does not." It is not much faith if we only trust God when things are going well and we feel close to him. Job's faith was real when in the midst of his sufferings he said, "Though he slay me, yet I will hope in him" (Job 13:15). Peter (I Peter 1:7) reminds his readers that the trials they face come "so that your faith—of greater value than gold...may be proved genuine and may result in praise, glory and honor when Jesus Christ is revealed."

Secondly, God also afflicts his servants **to glorify himself.** The whole creation, from angels to demons and everything in between looks at the strange thing God has done on this fallen planet in loving sinful, rebellious men and women and adopting them into his forever family. What could he be thinking to do that? But when these frail, half physical, half spiritual bipeds face troubles and trials and still trust and love God, he is glorified. When "suffering produces perseverance; perseverance, character; and character, hope," the Lord is honored (Romans 5:3-4). Spurgeon wrote, "We would never enjoy the juice of the grape if it were not trodden in the winepress nor feel the warmth of fire if the coals were not consumed. The wisdom and power of God are discovered through the trials which his children are permitted to pass."

Third, present afflictions **tend also to heighten future joy.** I remember a song I once heard, "God gave me a song that the angels cannot sing: I've been redeemed by the blood of the lamb." Because of the troubles and the sorrows of earth, I rejoice in God and his love even more. Peace is always sweeter after conflict. Rest is more welcome after a hard day's work. In a similar way will not the remembrance of our troubles here on earth enhance our joys in heaven?

When troubles come we must not let them make us bitter, but better, as we turn them into opportunities to grow in Christ likeness, to glorify God by taking them as from him and to look ahead with joy knowing that one day we will look back on all we have faced and see that all God did and allowed was for the best.

Be encouraged.

Something to ask yourself before you close this book today:

Which of the three reason listed why God lets troubles come our way means the most to you today? Why do you think so?

Biblical Virtues

To pray for your kids (whatever age they are)

I don't know where I first saw this. I just had a copy of it in my prayer notebook and I thought I would share it with you. I pray for our two children every day, though they are now in their 40's. Sometimes my prayers are pretty shallow and repetitive. It helps if I use one or two of these prayers each day.

1. **Salvation.** "Lord, let salvation spring up within my children, that they may obtain the salvation that is in Christ Jesus, with eternal glory' *(Is. 45:8, 2 Tim. 2:10).*

2. **Growth in grace.** "I pray that my children may grow in the grace and knowledge of our Lord and Savior Jesus Christ" *(2 Pet. 3:18).*

3. **Love.** "Grant, Lord, that my children may learn to live a life of love, through the Spirit who dwells in them" *(Gal. 5:25, Eph. 5:2).*

4. **Honesty and Integrity.** "May integrity and honesty be their virtue and their protection" *(Ps. 25:21).*

5. **Self-control.** "Father, help my children not to be like many others around then, but let them be alert and self-controlled in all they do" *(I Thes. 5:6).*

6. **Love for God's Word.** "May my children grow to find Your Word more precious than much pure gold and sweeter than honey from the comb" *(Ps. 19:10).*

7. **Justice.** "God, help my children to love justice as You do and act justly in all they do" *(Ps. 11:5, Mic. 6:8).*

8. **Mercy.** "May my children always be merciful, just as their heavenly Father is merciful" *(Lk.6:36).*

ENCOURAGE

9. **Respect (for self, others, authority).** "Father, grant that my children may show proper respect to everyone, as your Word commands" *(1 Pet. 2:17)*.

10. **Biblical self-esteem.** "Help my children develop a strong self-esteem that is rooted in the realization that they are God's workmanship, created in Christ Jesus" *(Eph. 2:10)*.

11. **Faithfulness.** "Let love and faithfulness never leave my children, but bind these twin virtues around their necks and write them on the tablet of their hearts" *(Prov. 3:3)*.

12. **Courage.** "May my children always be strong and courageous in their character and in their actions" *(Deut. 31:6)*.

13. **Purity.** "Create in them a pure heart, O God, and let that purity of heart be shown in their actions" *(Ps. 51:10)*.

14. **Kindness.** "Lord, may my children always try to be kind to each other and to everyone else" *(I Thes. 5:15)*.

15. **Generosity.** "Grant that my children may be generous and willing to share, and so lay-up treasure for themselves as a firm foundation for the coming age" *(I Tim. 6:18-19)*.

16. **Peace-loving.** "Father, let my children make every effort to do what leads to peace" *(Rom. 14:19)*.

17. **Joy.** "May my children be filled with the joy given by the Holy Spirit" *(I Thes. 1:6)*.

18. **Humility**. "God, please cultivate in my children the ability to show true humility toward all" *(Titus 3:2)*.

19. **Responsibility.** "Grant that my children may learn responsibility, for each one should carry his own load" *(Gal. 6:5)*.

20. **Compassion.** "Lord, please clothe my children with the virtue of compassion" *(Col. 3:12)*.

21. **Compassion.** "Lord, please clothe my children with the virtue of compassion" *(Col. 3:12)*.

22. **Responsibility.** "Grant that my children may learn responsibility, for each one should carry his own load" *(Gal. 6:5)*

23. **Contentment.** "Father, teach my children the secret of being content in any and every situation, through Him who gives them strength" *(Phil: 4:12-13)*.

24. **Faith.** "I pray that faith will find root and grow in my children's hearts, that by faith they may gain what has been promised to them" *(Luke 17:5-6, Heb. 11:1-40)*.

25. **A servant's heart.** "God, please help my children develop servants' hearts that they may serve wholeheartedly, as if they were serving the Lord, not men" *(Eph. 6:7)*.

26. **Hope.** "May the God of hope grant that my children may overflow with hope and hopefulness by the power of the Holy Spirit" *(Rom. 13:15)*.

27. **Willingness and ability to work.** "Teach my children, Lord, to value work and to work at it with all their heart, as work for the Lord, not for men" *(Col; 4:23)*.

28. **Passion for God.** "Lord, please instill in my children a soul that 'followeth hard after thee' *(Ps. 63:8)*, one that clings passionately to you."

29. **Self-discipline.** "Father, I pray that my children may acquire a disciplined and prudent life, doing what is right and just and fair" *(Prov. 1:3)*.

30. **Prayerfulness.** "Grant, Lord, that my children's lives may be marked by prayerfulness, that they may learn to pray in the spirit on all occasions with all kinds of prayers and requests" *(Eph. 6:18)*.

31. **Gratitude.** "Help my children to live lives that are always overflowing with thankfulness and always giving thanks to God the Father for everything, in the name of our Lord Jesus Christ *"(Eph. 5:20, Col 2:7)*.

ENCOURAGE

32. **A heart for missions.** "Lord, please help my children to develop a desire to see your glory declared among the nations, your marvelous deeds among all peoples" *(Ps. 6:3)*.

33. **Perseverance.** "Lord, teach my children perseverance in all they do, and help them especially to run with perseverance the race marked out for them" *(Heb. 12:1)*.

I hope you find this encouraging as you pray for your children.

Something to decide to do before you close this book today:

Photo copy these thirty prayers and try to use one or two of them to pray for your children every day.

God's Unscheduled Opportunities

The Lord said to Abram, "Leave your country, your people and your father's household and go to the land I will show you." Genesis 12:1

I am a fairly organized, plan-ahead person. Often I have things lined up pretty well. All is going smoothly and I think I have a handle on what's ahead, then comes one of life's interruptions. They can really throw me for a loop. But I have slowly come to realize that when my life is intersected by some dilemma or disaster, God is not a bit surprised. Every time he is able to so work out the interruption that it brings him glory and works for my good. Joe Stowell, in <u>Far From Home</u>, noted that God understands interruptions. *"...think of Jesus Christ, whose own glory in heaven was interrupted three years to be misunderstood, maligned and ultimately martyred on a rugged cross. All for the purpose of casting a victorious ray of light down through the centuries to my life and to yours."*

As you read the Bible you see people who have received well the interruptions God brought into their lives as they said, "God. I am willing to let you use this interruption to transition me to your intended purposes." And God used those interruptions to accomplish in and through them things far beyond themselves.

Think of what great things happened in and through lives that were interrupted: Abraham, Moses, Joseph, Job, Mary and Joseph and many more. In a sermon a pastor mused about what would have happened if Abraham had said, "I don't do trips." or if Noah has said, "I don't do boats." or Moses has said, "I don't do crowds." What if Joseph had said, "I don't do rescue operations in Egypt." or if Job had said, "I don't do sorrow," or if Mary had said no to the angel, or if Christ had said, "I don't do crosses," Where would we be today?

As hard as it can be, what the issue is when God lets/brings interruptions into our lives is to ask ourselves, "Am I willing to let this interruption in my life be used for things beyond myself--to be used for *His* glory, *His* gain, and *my* good?" Can we trust God enough to stop resisting life's interruptions and welcome them as his unscheduled opportunities? If God is sovereign that is the smartest thing to...though it still can be very difficult. That is one of the reasons Christians ask family and friends to pray for them when they are going through a tough time. We need one another. "Two are better than one and a threefold cord is hard to break."

Something to think about before you close this book today:

Picture missing your flight to your son or daughter's college graduation because TSA's security lines were so long...and you can't get your money back. Now reread these pages. What thoughts go through your mind? How do you picture you would be responding/reacting as you see your plane take off without you?

Attitude

Several years ago I saw a poster in a friend's office that really caught my attention. It was a quote by Chuck Swindoll titled "ATTITUDE." Chuck's thoughts made such an impression on me because they are so simple and obviously true. If they are put into practice, they can change our life, lead us to greater Christ-likeness and open us to all kinds of ministry opportunities. Through the years I also learned from my wife the value of choosing the right "attitude," So often I have seen her choose to have a positive attitude when I would have grumbled and complained. I've experienced what that positive attitude did for her and for those around her.

Here are Chuck's thoughts on "attitude."

This may shock you, but I believe the single most significant decision I can make on a day- to-day basis is my choice of attitude. It is more important than my past, my education, my bankroll, my successes or failures, fame or pain, what other people think of me, or say about me, my circumstances, or my position.

The attitude I choose keeps me going or cripples my progress. It alone fuels my fire or assaults my hope. When my attitudes are right, there's no barrier too high, no valley too deep, no dream too extreme, no challenge too great for me.

Yet we must admit that we spend more of our time concentrating and fretting over the things that can't be changed than we do giving attention to the one that we can change—our choice of attitude.

This particularly hit home with me one time in the middle of a move to a new city. We had taken a bunch of our stuff in our van to our new location. While we were there our realtor called and said the couple who were scheduled to close on our house in a few weeks now said they must sell their house first, which originally they had said they didn't need to do. So we put everything back in our van and brought it back to home.

There were a lot of different attitudes we could have had. Our life had been in a bit of turmoil for months and this capped it off. But as Swindoll said, our attitude is our choice. We chose to have a positive attitude. We didn't need to get mad at the people who changed their mind and caused us some inconvenience. Romans 8:28 is still true. God is still sovereign.

We did pretty well with our attitude about this and we did get a great note from our realtor that said, "I thank God for you in more ways than you could know. Having clients like you is a blessing to my job." Did that make us feel good! I think of what could have happened had we paid no attention to our attitude. Swindoll is right. So often we fret over things that we can't change. How much better to give attention to our attitude, something we can change. Choosing to have a positive attitude can enable us to better grab hold of the life that God has for us. Also it can cause others to take a closer look at our God.

Recently I have been reminded by a friend the need to choose to have a positive attitude and not let the negatives of the world wear me down. In a lot of the conversations with friends we find ourselves bemoaning the changes that have come to the United States in the last years. We see abortion on demand, a redefining of what marriage is, Christians morality not only thought of as old fashioned, but looked at as being evil, increased racial division, terrorism, politics dividing people more than ever…and the list goes on and on.

In the midst of one of these "aren't things terrible" conversations, one of the group said, "I have chosen to keep a positive attitude. I will not let all the things in the world turn me to living out of a negative attitude."

That caught my attention because listening to the daily news was causing in me fear, anger and frustration. Swindoll was right about the importance of a positive attitude.

Something to think about before you close this book today;
As you look ahead to today and this week, is your attitude what you need to live well for Christ? Remember your attitude is a choice. Also remember God is still sovereign in your life and the world.

A Leader's Prayer

Every once in a while someone asks me, "How do you like your new ministry of pastoring missionaries? My usual reply is something like this: What a privilege God has given Joy and me to be involved with these missionaries. They are a quality bunch of people and God is using them in wonderful ways. They are impacting for Christ and his Kingdom those they are working with. They are leaders equipping leaders.

So when I received a letter from my pastor that included a prayer for leaders, I thought of my missionary friends and every Christian whom God has called to lead. It comes from <u>Leadership Prayers</u> by Richard Kriegbaum: Tyndale House, 1998. May this prayer help you say to God what you need to say as you seek to live for Him in whatever leadership role he has given you.

Help me remember, God that I can be reassigned, neutralized or eliminated for a thousand different reasons at any moment. My leadership is precarious, hanging by the sliver thread of people's trust in me. Countless things over which I have no control can break that thread, including your call elsewhere, and I will be gone.

But they need a leader, and when I am gone they must have others to turn to, others whom they trust, who can tell them the truth. Show me those who can lead after me and better than me. Ruffle my spirit when they are near, quicken my heart when I feel their power, and open my eyes to see the special effect they have on people.

Protect me from preserving my own position or power or perspectives at the expense of future leaders. When they point out where I have not led well, shut my mouth and open my heart. Help me make it safe for them to try new things. Let me touch the spirit of those who possess the heart of a servant. I want to know them and love them and watch their energy flow into others around them. I want to claim them for this work and pray them into my place.

I will not have the privilege of choosing who will lead after me. Others will decide that. But I can help prepare leaders, and I can help the organization be ready for them

Show me the ones who challenge me, the ones with more freedom and stronger faith than I have. Point out the ones who love people better that I do, who lead because they really care about people. Make the spiritual giants visible to me. Let me notice the ones who attract loyal, high-quality friends.

Help me distinguish between the confident and the arrogant, between the humble and hesitant. Bring out the strong ones who can carry their own burdens and also the burdens of others. Allow tough times that will yield success to those who refuse to give up. Help me advance the leaders for the future.

Oh. God of mercy, don't let me stay in this job one day too long. And don't let this all fall apart after I leave.

I will not last forever, God. Where are my replacements?

Something you need to ask before you close this book today:

What part of this prayer jumped out at you and resonated with your heart?

Walking on Water

Most of us want to succeed in life as followers of Christ. We picture living a life that honors our Lord and of one day hearing him say to us, "Well done, good and faithful servant." But Jesus continually challenged people to move out of their comfort zones into new areas of growth. That is not easy because when we do that, failure of some kind is a real possibility. And we fear failure. There are good reasons why we do. Losers are not easily tolerated in our society. We fear becoming someone's laughing stock or making a fool of ourselves. We believe, mistakenly, that if we try and fail, it might be an unbearable burden.

We all fear failure to some degree, so often we either refuse to try to do something new or different or we set the goal so small trying to guarantee we won't fail. And what happens is we become stagnant in our lifestyles. We become afraid to venture out of our safe routines.

Life in this fallen world is a combination of successes and failures. If we never try anything, we will never fail, but also we will never succeed. God has not called us to become like hermits and never risk anything for his kingdom's sake. He challenges us to keep growing, to get out of the boat and walk with him on the water. Put yourself in Peter's place. The Lord is passing by. He's inviting you to go on the adventure of your life. But there is a storm out there. If you get out of the boat—whatever the boat is to you—you might sink. But if you don't get out of the boat, it is certain that you will never walk on the water with Jesus.

John Ortberg in <u>You Can't Walk On Water Unless You Get Out of The Boat,</u> noted that there is within us something or someone who is telling us that there is more to life than staying safely in the boat. If you step up to the plate, you might strike out. Yes, but if you don't step up to the plate, you will never know what it is like to get a hit, to maybe even hit a home run. Babe Ruth struck out 1330 times, but he also hit 714 home runs.

ENCOURAGE

Jonas Salk developed a vaccine for polio but only after two hundred unsuccessful attempts. Someone asked him, "How did it feel to fail two hundred times?" He replied, "I did not fail two hundred times. I just discovered two hundred ways how not to vaccinate for polio."

Was Babe Ruth a failure or Jonas Salk? Did Peter fail? I guess he did, in a sense. He did take his eyes off Jesus and look at the waves, but there were eleven bigger failures in the boat. They failed quietly, uncriticized. Only Peter knew public failure.

John Ortberg pointed out that only Peter knew two other things. Only he knew what it was like by faith to get out of the boat and walk on water, to know the glory of trusting Jesus' call and by God's power doing what no one else had ever done. And secondly, only Peter knew the glory of being lifted up by Jesus in a moment of desperate need and learning that Jesus is wholly adequate to save. The others couldn't know those things because they didn't even get out of the boat. The worse failure is not to sink in the waves, but to never get out of the boat.

Be encouraged.

Something you need to ask today before you close this book:

Where is God asking you to join him and "walk on water"? What is keeping you from "getting out of the boat"? Write your thoughts here. Tell someone today what you wrote down.

Abide with Me

I hope that you, like I, can appreciate both the old hymns and the new worship songs. I have younger friends who can't stand those old hymns especially when they are played by that loud, awful sounding musical instrument called a pipe organ. I have older friends who think the new songs are shallow and of no help to worship. They call them 7-11 songs: seven words repeated eleven times.

There is bad music and bad lyrics in both categories. All old hymns aren't great. Research shows that out of hundreds of hymns in most hymnals only a little over one hundred are ever used. I've sung new songs in some contemporary worship services that I'm sure won't be used ten years from now, if even next year. Why have and will some hymns/songs stay popular for centuries? I'm sure the tunes help, but it is the words that touch the heart.

Today I read a hymn I have often sung that was written 163 years ago. I realized why it is still popular. I thought I'd share with you some of my thoughts as I read it.

Abide with me! Fast falls the eventide. The darkness deepens; Lord, with me abide! When other helpers fail and comforts flee, help of the helpless, O abide with me!

Recently I have talked with people who have faced some real darkness, in their work, in their families and personally. Counselors have helped…a little. Friends' advice has sometimes been a hindrance not a help. The darkness has deepened. Is there help available? Yes, always. The Lord will always be there and he especially is a help to the helpless.

Swift to its close ebbs out life's little day. Earth's joys grow dim; its glories pass away. Change and decay in all around I see. O Thou who changes not, abide with me!

The middle aged author of these words was dying of TB. How good it is to know that no matter what changes take place in our lives, our families,

ENCOURAGE

our ministry or our country, there is One who changes not, whose promises are sure, who loves us and who will never leave us.

I need Thy presence every passing hour. What but Thy grace can foil the tempter's power? Who, like Thyself, my guide and stay can be? Through cloud and sunshine, Lord, abide with me.

What a good reminder this is that not just every day, but every hour we need God's grace to guide and strengthen. I think that is what it means to pray without ceasing. We don't just talk to God in our morning Quiet Time and then go through the day with the spiritual strength we got then. Also how insightful that we do need God's presence in both the cloudy times and the sunny days. And how wonderful that he is always there to abide with us.

I fear no foe. With Thee at hand to bless; ills have no weight, and tears no bitterness. Where is death's sting? Where, grave, thy victory? I triumph still, if Thou abide with me.

In this fallen world there are many foes. Some are real people in our lives, some who are evil and others who hurt us just because they themselves have been impacted by the sin of the world. Some foes are aspects of nature, accidents, sickness, earthquakes, floods. These come because this world is not what God created it to be. There are persecution, misunderstanding, and the lack of resources. Then there is death. But God has promised that he will work all things together for the good of those who love him. Of course there are foes, ills, tears and even death. But with God abiding with us, their oppressive weight, their bitterness and deadly sting are gone. We know that one day in his presence we will look back on what he has allowed to hit us in this life and say that Romans 8:28 was true and realize that God does/did all things well.

You can see why I still like some of those old hymns. The language may be a bit King James-ish, but, wow, the depth of the thoughts. I hope this old hymn has encouraged you as it did me.

Something to think about before you close this book today: Which of the four verses of the hymn speaks most clearly to you today? Thank God for the truth in that verse.

ENCOURAGE

Plenteous Redemption

Sometimes at Sunday worship, when the monthly or quarterly communion elements are majestically in place, I instinctively have a fleeting sense of disappointment: the sermon will be cut short. And, sadly, the communion service often becomes just a ritual. I needed help so that the Lord's Supper could be to me what Christ intended.

Happily once at a weekly meeting I attend, called, "The Dead Theologian's Society," we studied, *God is Love*, a book of communion addresses by J. W. Alexander, circa 1850. These sermons have helped me look much more deeply at the Lord's Supper and helped me not to fall into the trap of just going through the ritual.

One sermon was from Psalm 130:7 *"...and with him is plenteous redemption."(*KJV*)* Often I take my redemption for granted and don't think of it as big as it is. Alexander reminded me how incredible it is. In the Old Testament, redemption was, "a ransom paid for our freedom... the buying back from slavery, the deliverance from merciless oppression." That reminded me of why I needed redemption: I was reminded what it was like to be "conquered and sold under sin," and what it was like before I came to Christ to be under God's wrath. "Death, temporal, spiritual and eternal had begun to seize upon us." (I remember, as a youth, how I wondered where I'd go when I died.) Happily, in 1958, I *was* redeemed, delivered "from all the evils of the fall, by the incarnation, work and sufferings of our only Mediator, the Lord Jesus Christ."

When I paused to meditate on what redemption meant and means to me and the cost it was to Christ, I praised God for his love with my refreshed insight.

But eagerly, I and the group read on. Alexander focused on the word *plenteous. (*How many times recently have you used *that* word?) Alexander listed six ways our redemption is plenteous.

He pointed out that our redemption is plenteous "... because it introduces us to all the abundance of inconceivable good." He then noted some of that good. He pointed out that by redemption we are not just "set free from prison" (that would be wonderful) but amazingly we are admitted to "the palace of our King!" The prodigal son was "not only seen afar off, and met, and admitted; he was kissed, clothed, beautified and feasted." Now that's rich, exciting imagery. Further, "The Bride, the Lamb's wife, was not merely freed from the cords and humiliations and duress of her long captivity; (she would have been satisfied with that) she was decked with jewels and installed in all the royalties of her Divine Husband." To change the imagery, "The slave is lifted to a throne." This is not just redemption we have, but *plenteous redemption*.

Alexander then listed thirteen blessings we can enjoy. "Here on this side of the river are the joys of pardon, the spirit of adoption, in many the assurance of God's love, power over the world, perseverance in grace, the gradual but certain augmentation of inward holiness, the ripe fruits of knowledge, the heavenly wine of communion, the delights of devotion, the lifting up of soul in psalmody and praise, the fellowship of mutual love, the foretaste of glory and the serene departure to full emancipation."

Alexander's extravagantly rich, poetic language is not the way we speak today, *(we should have such facility)*, but there are meaningful thoughts in them. I would encourage you to take some time to look at that last quote and think about each of those images of blessing which are available to us. You will, as did I, praise God again for his love, his plenteous redemption.

Then, Dr. Alexander listed the blessings of our *plenteous redemption* on the other side of our mortal sojourn: "angelic welcome, triumph in the Judgment, the sight of the Son of Man in his glory, acquittal by his voice, a place at his right hand, a seat on his throne, and an eternal vision of his infinite and divine beauty." Take some time and meditate on those blessings ahead of us. "For this, and unto this, we are redeemed: and is it not then, *plenteous redemption?*" Oh, yes!

Whatever trials and struggles you and I may be going through now, we can be *encouraged* when we dwell on the *plenteous redemption* that Christ has purchased for us; thus, in a new way, we will rediscover the love in the heart of God for us. Anticipated blessings will be revealed. I've found it so.

May we know more and more of our plenteous redemption.

Something to do before you close this book today:

Look again at the thirteen blessings on this side of the river that Alexander listed. Write down three that today mean the most to you. Think about why they do?